98 Mocktail Recipes: Delicious Non-Alcoholic Drinks for Every Occasion

Bold Bites

Copyright © 2023 Bold Bites
All rights reserved.
:

Contents

INTRODUCTION 7
1. Blueberry Breeze 8
2. Fruit Fiesta 8
3. Cranberry Citrus Punch 9
4. Melon Mango Mocktail 10
5. Blue Lagoon 11
6. Midnight Margarita 11
7. Watermelon Refresher 12
8. Fizzy Raspberry Punch 13
9. Mango Delight 14
10. Ginger Citrus Cooler 14
11. Chunky Monkey 15
12. Apple Berry Fix 16
13. Peachy Punch 16
14. Colada Delight 17
15. Cucumber Limeade 18
16. Strawberry Swirl 19
17. Shamrock Shake 20
18. Passion Fruit Punch 21
19. Melon Lime Slushy 22
20. Orange Sunrise 22
21. Luscious Lemonade 23
22. Cherry Pineapple Refresher 24
23. Mango Mint Julep 24
24. Pina Calada Smoothie 25
25. Cranberry Fizz 26
26. Chocolate Mocha Freeze 27
27. Strawberry Shortcake 27

28. Peachy Citrus Surprise 28
29. Island Breeze 29
30. Pomegranate Lemonade 30
31. Cranberry Sipper 31
32. Apricot Sunrise 32
33. Kiwi Mojito 32
34. Cucumber Mint Fizz 33
35. Tropical Dream 34
36. Lemon Meringue Freeze 35
37. Honeydew Breeze 35
38. Pink Paradise 36
39. Cinnamon Punch 37
40. Grapefruit Zinger 38
41. Party Punch 38
42. Peachy Sunrise 39
43. Sweet Tangerine Treat 40
44. Pina Colada Float 41
45. Mango Tango 42
46. Melon Punch 43
47. Banana Banana Shake 43
48. Orange Dream Swirl 44
49. Apple Slammer 45
50. Strawberry Breeze 46
51. Cherry Limeade 47
52. Raspberry Sunrise 47
53. Tutti Frutti Twist 48
54. Mocktail Margarita 49
55. Blueberry Limeade 50
56. Pear Sorbet Float 51

57. Peachy Green Cooler 52

58. Raspberry Fizz 52

59. Elderflower Freeze 53

60. Passion Fruit Frappe 54

61. Orange Crush 55

62. Mojito Popsicle 56

63. Peach Breeze 56

64. Mango Margarita 57

65. Strawberry Cream Soda 58

66. Banana Sunrise 59

67. Blueberry Blast 59

68. Apple and Cranberry Cooler 60

69. Mock Mai Tai 61

70. Orange Grapefruit Punch 62

71. Melon Splash 62

72. Creamy Coconut Float 63

73. Honeydew Lemonade 64

74. Blueberry Mojito 65

75. Ginger Honey Cooler 65

76. Pineapple Breeze 66

77. Cranberry Zinger 67

78. Watermelon Granita 68

79. Raspberry Coconut Cooler 68

80. Orange Dream Punch 69

81. Fruity Sangria 70

82. Berry Breeze 71

83. Spiced Apricot Refresher 72

84. Key Lime Pie 72

85. Citrus Cooler 73

86. Kiwi Margarita 74
87. Margarita Punch 75
88. Peach n' Cream 76
89. Mango Sunrise 77
90. Cranberry Swizzle 77
91. Honeydew Limeade 78
92. Apricot Fizz 79
93. Lemon Coconut Refresher 79
94. Fruity Freeze 80
95. Green Apple Slush 81
96. Raspberry Peach Slush 82
97. Banana Colada 83
98. Pomegranate Punch 83
CONCLUSION 85

INTRODUCTION

Welcome to the world of mocktails! Mocktails are the perfect way to enjoy the delicious flavor of a festive drink without the worry of alcohol. With 98 Refreshing Mocktail Recipes: Delicious Non-Alcoholic Drinks for Every Occasion, you will never have to miss out on the fun.

In this cookbook, you will find recipes to make delicious and unique non-alcoholic drinks to fit any occasion. From Bloody Marys to Margaritas, Pina Coladas to classic Italian Sodas, you can easily make sure that everyone at the party can join in on the fun. Not only will these drinks look elegant when served, but you'll also impress your guests with the flavor.

You'll also learn about different types of ingredients and techniques to help you create the perfect mocktails like mastering how to make flavorful syrups and simple syrups, as well as how to give them the perfect carbonation. With this cookbook, you can explore a world of drinks that are sure to become a hit at any gathering.

To help you get started, we included an introduction to mocktails with an overview of the basics. We will take you through the process of gathering ingredients, various techniques, and the proper procedure for creating a delicious drink. With this cookbook, you'll be able to make drinks that rival the professional bartenders with ease.

So, join us as we explore the exciting world of delicious mocktails. With the recipes and tips in 98 Refreshing Mocktail Recipes: Delicious Non-Alcoholic Drinks for Every Occasion, you'll be able to bring any event to life with a memorable experience. From holiday gatherings to family dinner parties, you will be sure to make your friends and family happy with a special drink that everyone can enjoy. Let's begin your new journey into the wonderful world of mocktails!

1. Blueberry Breeze

Blueberry Breeze is a delicious smoothie treat that is perfect for any summer day. Bursting with nutrition and flavor, this smoothie is both healthy and refreshing.

Serving: 1 | Preparation Time: 5 minutes | Ready Time: 5 minutes

Ingredients:
-1/2 cup frozen blueberries
-1/2 cup almond milk
-1/4 teaspoon vanilla extract
-1/4 teaspoon ground cinnamon
-3-4 ice cubes

Instructions:
1. In a blender, add all the ingredients (blueberries, almond milk, vanilla extract, ground cinnamon, and ice cubes).
2. Blend until desired consistency is reached.
3. Pour the smoothie into a glass, enjoy it immediately.

Nutrition information:
Calories: 80
Fat: 1.5g
Carbohydrates: 14g
Protein: 2g

2. Fruit Fiesta

Fruit Fiesta is a vibrant, colorful, and delicious dessert made up of a combination of fresh fruits in a sugary custard. Serve it to friends and family as a delicious brunch item or afternoon snack.

Serving: 8-10 | Preparation Time: 20 minutes | Ready Time: 1 hour

Ingredients:
- 4 cups of sliced fresh fruit of your choice (pineapple, peaches, kiwi, etc)
- 1 cup of light brown sugar

- 1/2 teaspoon of ground vanilla
- 2 large eggs
- 1/4 teaspoon of salt
- 2 cups of heavy cream
- 2 tablespoons of butter

Instructions:
1. Preheat your oven to 350F (175°C). Grease an 8 or 9-inch baking dish with butter.
2. Combine the sliced fruit of your choice with brown sugar, vanilla, eggs, salt, and cream. Mix until everything is evenly combined.
3. Pour the mixture into the prepared baking dish and spread evenly. Dot with butter.
4. Bake for 45 minutes to 1 hour, or until the custard is golden brown.

Nutrition information (per serving):
- Calories: 370
- Fat: 16g
- Carbs: 42g
- Protein: 5g

3. Cranberry Citrus Punch

Cranberry Citrus Punch is a refreshing and delicious beverage perfect for any occasion.

Serving: 6 | Preparation Time: 5 mins | Ready Time: 5 mins

Ingredients:
* 1 12-ounce can frozen cranberry juice concentrate
* 1 12-ounce can frozen lemonade or limeade concentrate
* 6 cups cold water
* 1 1/2 cups chilled orange juice
* 1 cup chilled pineapple juice

Instructions:
1. In a large pitcher, stir together cranberry juice concentrate and lemonade or limeade concentrate.

2. Gradually stir in water, orange juice and pineapple juice.
3. Serve chilled.

Nutrition information (per 1/2 cup):
* Calories: 95
* Total Fat: 0g
* Sodium: 5mg
* Potassium: 90mg
* Total Carbohydrates: 24g
* Protein: 0g

4. Melon Mango Mocktail

This sparkling treat features the sweet and fragrant flavors of melon and mango and is topped off with a kiss of fizz. In addition to being incredibly delicious and easy to make, this melon mango mocktail is also incredibly healthy and refreshing.

Serving: 1 drink | Preparation Time: 5 minutes | Ready Time: 10 minutes

Ingredients:
- 1/2 cup cubed honeydew melon
- 1/2 cup cubed mango
- 1 teaspoon honey
- 1/2 cup sparkling water

Instruction:
1. In a bowl, mash the honeydew and mango together until well blended.
2. Pour the honey over the melon and mango and stir until evenly incorporated.
3. Pour the melon and mango mixture into a glass, add the sparkling water and stir until combined.
4. Enjoy!

Nutrition information:
Calories: 118, Total Fat: 0g, Sodium: 11mg, Total Carbohydrates: 29g, Protein: 2g, Vitamin A: 26%, Vitamin C: 63%, Calcium: 4%, Iron: 2%.

5. Blue Lagoon

Blue Lagoon is an easy, delicious and flavorful smoothie made with fresh blueberries and other ingredients. Enjoy it as a snack or a refreshing breakfast drink.

Serving: 2| Preparation Time: 5 minutes | Ready Time: 5 minutes

Ingredients:
-1/2 cup frozen blueberries
-1/4 cup frozen mango
-1/4 cup pineapple chunks
-1 cup almond milk
-1/2 teaspoon honey
-4-5 ice cubes

Instructions:
1. Place all ingredients in a blender.
2. Blend on high power until smooth.
3. Pour into glasses and enjoy.

Nutrition information:
Serving Size : 2 Cups
Calories : 117 calories
Protein : 2.2 grams
Carbs : 24.2 grams
Fat : 2.02 grams

6. Midnight Margarita

The Midnight Margarita is a delicious twist on the classic Margarita. It combines Jose Cuervo tequila, Cointreau, and lime juice with a blackberry and vanilla simple syrup for a sophisticated flavor balance.

Serving: 4| Preparation Time: 15 minutes| Ready Time: 2 hours

Ingredients:

- 2 oz Jose Cuervo tequila
- 1 oz Cointreau
- 1 oz fresh lime juice
- 2 teaspoons blackberry and vanilla simple syrup, divided
- 2 tablespoons coarse sugar
- 1/4 cup fresh blackberries, smashed
- Salt

Instructions:
1. Rim 4 glasses with coarse sugar.
2. In a cocktail shaker, combine tequila, Cointreau, lime juice, and 1 teaspoon of the blackberry and vanilla simple syrup. Shake vigorously and strain into the glasses.
3. To the shaker, add the smashed blackberries and remaining simple syrup. Shake vigorously and strain into the glasses over the margarita.
4. Garnish with a blackberry and salt rim.

Nutrition information:
Calories: 145, Total Fat: 0g, Sodium: 2mg, Total Carbohydrates: 9g, dietary fiber: 0g, Sugars: 8g, Protein: 0g

7. Watermelon Refresher

This refreshing Watermelon Refresher is perfect for a hot summer day. A combination of watermelon and lime flavors will tantalize your tastebuds and leave you wanting more.

Serving: 4| Preparation Time: 10 minutes| Ready Time: 10 minutes

Ingredients:
- 1 cup diced watermelon
- 1/2 lime, juiced and zested
- 1/4 cup sugar
- 2 cups of water

Instructions:

1. In a medium bowl, combine diced watermelon, lime juice and zest, and sugar.
2. Using a muddler, muddle the ingredients together until the sugar is dissolved and the watermelon starts to break apart.
3. Pour in the water and use a spoon to combine everything.
4. Strain the watermelon refresher into glasses over ice.

Nutrition information Per Serving (1 cup):
Calories: 86, Fat: 0.1g, Saturated Fat: 0.0g, Sodium: 2mg, Carbohydrates: 22.2g, Fiber: 0.4g, Sugar: 16.3g, Protein: 0.9g

8. Fizzy Raspberry Punch

Fizzy Raspberry Punch is a sweet and delicious treat perfect for any occasion. It's easy to make and loaded with raspberry flavor and a hint of citrus.

Serving: 10-12 | Preparation Time: 5 minutes | Ready Time: 5 minutes

Ingredients:
-1 liter of carbonated raspberry-grapefruit soda
-1 pint of fresh raspberries
-1 half cup of vodka (optional)
-Ice cubes
-Sliced orange, for garnish

Instructions:
1. In a punch bowl or pitcher, combine soda, raspberries, and vodka (if using).
2. Stir to combine.
3. Add ice cubes and garnish with orange slices.
4. Serve immediately.

Nutrition information (per serving):
Calories: 90, Carbohydrates: 17g, Protein: 1g, Fat: 0g

9. Mango Delight

Mango Delight is a light and fluffy dessert dish made with fresh mangoes, skimmed milk, honey, and cardamom. Enjoy the unique flavours and textures of this traditional Indian delicacy!

Serving: 4-6 | Preparation Time: 20 minutes | Ready Time: 50 minutes

Ingredients:
- 2 mangos, peeled and cubed
- 2 cups of skimmed milk
- 2 tablespoons of honey
- 1 teaspoon of cardamom

Instructions:
1. Preheat oven to 375 degrees F.
2. In a bowl, mix together mango cubes, milk, honey and cardamom, and blend until smooth.
3. Grease a baking pan with butter and pour in the mango mixture.
4. Bake for 35 minutes.
5. Let cool before serving.

Nutrition information:
Serving size: 1/6 of dish
Calories: 220
Fat: 0.5g
Cholesterol: 1.5mg
Sodium: 70mg
Carbohydrates: 50g
Protein: 5g

10. Ginger Citrus Cooler

This Ginger Citrus Cooler is the perfect combination of sweet and tangy, with an unexpected zip of ginger. With a refreshing blend of fresh citrus and coconut water, this drink will surely be a hit at any summer gathering.

Serving: 4 | Preparation Time: 10 minutes | Ready Time: 10 minutes

Ingredients:
- 2 large oranges
- 2 large limes
- 1/2 cup coconut water
- 1/4 cup agave nectar
- 3 tablespoons freshly grated ginger
- 1/2 teaspoon kosher salt

Instructions:
1. Cut oranges and limes into wedges and spiral wedges on 4 glasses.
2. In a medium mixing bowl, combine the coconut water, agave nectar, grated ginger, and salt. Stir until well blended.
3. Divide the mixture among the 4 glasses, then top off with ice cubes and a few orange or lime slices for garnish.

Nutrition information: Per serving. Calories 95, Fat 0g, Cholesterol 0mg, Sodium 175mg, Carbohydrates 25g, Protein 1g.

11. Chunky Monkey

Chunky Monkey is a classic ice cream sundae recipe made with bananas, chocolate chunks, and whipped cream. It is a delectable summer treat that is sure to please all ages.

Serving: 4-6 | Preparation Time: 10 minutes | Ready Time: 10 minutes

Ingredients:
- 1 banana, sliced
- 2 tablespoons semi-sweet chocolate chips
- 4 scoops of vanilla ice cream
- 2 tablespoons whipped cream

Instructions:
1. Slice the banana into thin pieces and place on a plate.
2. Sprinkle the chocolate chips over the banana slices.

3. Place two scoops of ice cream per person on top of the banana slices and chocolate chips.
4. Squirt the whipped cream on top of the ice cream.
5. Serve immediately.

Nutrition information: Each serving of Chunky Monkey contains approximately 120 calories, 4 grams of fat, and 16 grams of sugar.

12. Apple Berry Fix

Apple Berry Fix is a delicious and healthy side dish made with a mix of fresh apples and berries. With just a few ingredients, this simple recipe is ready in minutes and is full of antioxidants, natural sweetness, and a hint of cinnamon. Serve it as a breakfast side or as a snack throughout the day.

Serving: 4 | Preparation Time: 5 minutes | Ready Time: 10 minutes

Ingredients:
- 2 tart apples (such as Granny Smith), chopped
- 2 cups fresh or frozen berries (such as raspberries, blueberries, and blackberries)
- 2 tablespoons honey
- 1 teaspoon of ground Cinnamon

Instructions:
1. In a medium bowl, combine the chopped apples and berries.
2. Drizzle with honey and sprinkle with ground cinnamon.
3. Stir until the mixture is completely coated with honey and cinnamon.
4. Serve immediately or refrigerate for up to two hours.

Nutrition information (per serving):
Calories: 145 | Total Fat: 0g | Sodium: 6.7mg | Carbohydrates: 37.7g | Dietary Fiber: 6.1g | Protein: 0.7g

13. Peachy Punch

Peachy Punch is a light and tasty summer drink that is sure to be a hit at any gathering! This refreshing beverage is packed with a mix of fresh fruit flavors, plus a special secret ingredient.

Serving: Serves 4 | Preparation Time: 5 minutes | Ready Time: 20 minutes

Ingredients:
- 2 cups of water
- 4 cups of orange juice
- 2 cups of peach nectar
- 2 tablespoons of honey
- 1 teaspoon of grated ginger
- 1 tablespoon of lime juice
- 1 teaspoon of vanilla extract

Instructions:
1. In a large pitcher, mix together the water, orange juice, peach nectar, honey, and grated ginger.
2. Refrigerate for 15 minutes to allow the flavors to meld.
3. Just before serving, stir in the fresh lime juice and vanilla extract.
4. Serve chilled over ice.

Nutrition information:
Calories: 136 kcal, Carbohydrates: 33 g, Protein: 1 g, Fat: 0 g, Saturated Fat: 0 g, Cholesterol: 0 mg, Sodium: 4 mg, Potassium: 268 mg, Fiber: 0 g, Sugar: 28 g, Vitamin A: 133 IU, Vitamin C: 64 mg, Calcium: 27 mg, Iron: 0.4 mg

14. Colada Delight

Colada Delight is an irresistibly fruity dessert that is sure to be a hit at any party. With a delectable combination of pineapple, cream of coconut, and strawberry flavors, this crowd-pleasing dessert is sure to tantalize your taste buds.

Serving: 8-10 | Preparation Time: 10 minutes | Ready Time: 2 hours

Ingredients:
- 1 1/2 cups pineapple juice
- 1 can cream of coconut
- 1 pint fresh strawberries, hulled and sliced
- 2 packages vanilla pudding mix
- 4 cups of cold whole milk

Instructions:
1. In a large bowl, whisk together the pineapple juice, cream of coconut, and vanilla pudding mix until smooth.
2. Slowly whisk in the cold milk until the pudding mixture is thick and creamy.
3. Gently fold in the hulled, sliced strawberries.
4. Pour the mixture into individual serving dishes or into one large dish, cover with plastic wrap, and chill in the refrigerator for at least 2 hours.

Nutrition information:
Calories: 130; Total Fat: 4.5g; Sodium: 260mg; Total Carbohydrates: 22g; Protein: 2g.

15. Cucumber Limeade

Cucumber Limeade is an incredibly refreshing and deliciously light drink that will be perfect for those hot summer days. It's perfect for a casual gathering or for an outdoor BBQ. It's easy to make with just a few ingredients, and you'll be sure to impress your friends and family.

Serving : 8 | Preparation Time : 15 minutes | Ready Time : 15 minutes

Ingredients :
- 3 cups water
- 2 cups cucumbers, peeled and diced
- 2 tablespoons lime juice
- 1/4 cup honey
- Ice

Instructions :
1. In a medium saucepan, bring 2 cups of the water to a boil.

2. Add the cucumbers and simmer for 10 minutes.
3. Remove from heat and let cool.
4. Add the lime juice, honey, and the remaining 1 cup of water to the saucepan and stir to combine.
5. Strain the mixture through a fine mesh sieve.
6. Add the cucumber limeade to a pitcher and stir in ice.
7. Serve and enjoy!

Nutrition information : Per Serving (about 1 cup): Calories: 30, Fat: 0g, Cholesterol: 0mg, Sodium: 5mg, Carbohydrates: 8g Sugars: 7g, Protein: 0g.

16. Strawberry Swirl

This delicious and sweet Strawberry Swirl combines a rich cream cheese base with a strawberry topping for a unique treat that is perfect for any occasion. This dish serves six and takes about 30 minutes to prepare, with an additional 15 minutes for baking.

Serving: 6| Preparation Time: 30 minutes| Ready Time: 45 minutes

Ingredients:
- 1 box of yellow cake mix
- 2 eggs
- 1/3 cup of vegetable oil
- 1 package (8 oz.) cream cheese
- 1/2 cup of sugar
- 1 teaspoon of vanilla
- 2 tablespoons of flour
- 1 1/2 cups of fresh, sliced strawberries
- 1 tablespoon of sugar

Instructions:
1. Preheat oven to 350 degrees Fahrenheit and lightly grease a 9-inch springform pan.
2. In a large bowl, combine the cake mix, eggs, and oil. Beat until smooth.
3. Pour the cake mix batter into the springform pan and spread evenly.

4. In a separate bowl, beat cream cheese until smooth. Add sugar, vanilla, and flour and mix until combined. Spread on top of cake mix layer.
5. Place the sliced strawberries on top of the cream cheese layer and sprinkle sugar over the top.
6. Bake for 15 minutes. Let cool completely before serving.

Nutrition information:
Serving Size: Per one slice
Calories: 295
Fat: 13 g
Carbohydrates: 37 g
Protein: 3 g
Sodium: 265 mg

17. Shamrock Shake

Make this classic treat from McDonald's, the Shamrock Shake. A creamy and minty shake that's sure to satisfy your St. Patrick's day sweet tooth.

Servings: 4| Preparation Time: 5 minutes| Ready Time: 5 minutes

Ingredients:
- 2 cups vanilla ice cream
- 1 cup whole milk
- 1/2 teaspoon mint extract
- 1/4 teaspoon green food coloring
- 2 tablespoons chocolate syrup
- Whipped cream (optional)
- 1 tablespoon rainbow sprinkles (optional)

Instructions:
1. In a blender, combine the vanilla ice cream, milk, mint extract, and food coloring.
2. Blend until smooth.
3. Divide the shake between four glasses.
4. Top with a generous amount of chocolate syrup, whipped cream and rainbow sprinkles.

Nutrition information:
Calories: 234, Protein: 5g, Fat: 14g, Carbohydrates: 23g

18. Passion Fruit Punch

Passion Fruit Punch is a deliciously sweet and tangy drink perfect for any occasion! Perfect for summer days, this punch is made with simple yet tasty ingredients. Served chilled, this punch can be ready in just 10 minutes.

Serving: 6-8 people | Preparation Time: 5 minutes | Ready Time: 10 minutes

Ingredients:
- 2 1/2 cups passion fruit juice
- 1 cup pineapple juice
- 2 tablespoons lime juice
- 2 tablespoons sugar
- 1 cup seltzer water
- 1 lime, sliced

Instructions:
1. In a large pitcher, combine the passion fruit juice, pineapple juice, lime juice, and sugar.
2. Stir until the sugar is dissolved.
3. Add the seltzer water and stir to combine.
4. Add a few slices of lime to the punch for extra flavor.
5. Serve chilled.

Nutrition information:
Calories: 55 kcal
Carbohydrates: 13 g
Protein: 0.4 g
Fat: 0.3 g
Sodium: 7 mg

19. Melon Lime Slushy

This refreshing Melon Lime Slushy is the perfect summertime quencher. Tangy and sweet, this slushy is a great way to cool down while still enjoying a delicious treat.

Serving: 4 | Preparation Time: 5 minutes| Ready Time: 10 minutes

Ingredients:
- 1 honeydew melon, peeled, seeded and cubed
- 2 limes, juiced
- 3 tablespoons white sugar
- 2 cups cold water
- Crushed ice

Instructions:
1. In a blender, combine the honeydew cubes, lime juice, and sugar. Mix until blended.
2. Pour in cold water and blend until completely combined.
3. Add 2 cups of crushed ice and blend until the contents become a slushy texture.
4. Divide the slushy into four glasses and serve immediately.

Nutrition information:
Calories: 132 kcal, Total Fat: 0.3 g, Saturated Fat: 0 g, Trans Fat: 0 g, Cholesterol: 0 mg, Sodium: 5 mg, Carbohydrate: 33 g, Fiber: 2 g, Sugar: 25 g, Protein: 2.1 g

20. Orange Sunrise

Orange Sunrise is a delicious and refreshing drink perfect for the summer months. It combines citrusy orange juice and tart cranberry juice with vodka, making a light and tasty cocktail.

Serving: 1 | Preparation Time: 5 minutes| Ready Time: 5 minutes

Ingredients:
- 2 oz vodka

- 4 oz freshly-squeezed orange juice
- 2 oz cranberry juice
- Orange slices, for garnish (optional)

Instructions:
1. In a shaker filled with ice, combine the vodka, orange juice and cranberry juice.
2. Shake vigorously until combined and chilled.
3. Strain into a chilled glass, such as a martini glass, and garnish with orange slices.

Nutrition information:
Calories: 120 kcal, Carbohydrates: 8.4 g, Protein: 0.4 g, Fat: 0.1 g, Sodium: 4.7 mg, Sugar: 6.4 g.

21. Luscious Lemonade

This Luscious Lemonade recipe will have you feeling refreshed and cool on a hot summer day. With just a few ingredients and minimal time, you can whip up this delicious homemade lemonade in no time.

Serving: Makes 8 servings. | Preparation Time: 5 minutes. | Ready Time: 5 minutes.

Ingredients:
- 1 cup white sugar
- 1 cup freshly squeezed lemon juice
- 8 cups water
- Ice cubes

Instruction:
1. In a medium bowl, stir together the sugar and lemon juice until the sugar is dissolved.
2. Pour this mixture into a large pitcher and add the water. Stir until well blended.
3. Chill the lemonade for an hour or two until it is icy cold.
4. Fill 8 glasses with ice cubes, pour the lemonade over the ice, and garnish with wedges of lemon.

Nutrition information: Calories 90, Total Fat 0g, Cholesterol 0mg, Sodium 4mg, Total Carbs 24g, Sugars 24g, Protein 0g.

22. Cherry Pineapple Refresher

Cherry Pineapple Refresher is a delicious, fruity and refreshing twist on iced tea. It's perfect for sipping on a hot summer day, sure to quench your thirst.

Serving: Makes 1 serving| Preparation Time: 5 minutes| Ready Time: 5 minutes

Ingredients:
- 2 cups chilled brewed white tea
- 1/2 cup cherry-pineapple juice
- 2 ounces brandy
- 2 tablespoons agave syrup
- Dash of grenadine

Instructions:
1. In a glass, combine cherry-pineapple juice, brandy, agave syrup, and grenadine.
2. Fill glass with ice and brewed white tea.
3. Stir until all ingredients are combined.
4. Garnish with a cherry and pineapple wheel.

Nutrition information:
Calories: 210, Fat: 0 g, Saturated Fat: 0g, Sodium: 5mg, Carbohydrates 22g, Dietary Fiber:0g, Protein: 0g

23. Mango Mint Julep

Sweet and refreshing, Mango Mint Juleps are a perfect summertime beverage. This unique combination of tart and creamy mango, herbal mint and tangy lime juice, topped with sparkling water makes for a delightful and delicious treat.

Serving: 6 | Preparation Time: 10 minutes | Ready Time: 10 minutes

Ingredients:
– 3/4 cup of freshly squeezed lime juice
– 1 mango, peeled and diced
– 10-12 fresh mint leaves, finely chopped
– 1/4 cup of sugar
– 6 cups of sparkling water

Instructions:
1. In a blender, combine the lime juice, mango, mint and sugar. Blend until smooth.
2. Pour the mixture into 6 glasses filled with ice.
3. Top each glass with 1 cup of sparkling water.
4. Stir to combine and garnish with extra mint leaves, if desired.

Nutrition information:
Serving size: 1 glass
Calories: 80
Fat: 0g
Carbohydrate: 19g
Protein: 0g

24. Pina Calada Smoothie

This delicious, creamy Pina Colada Smoothie will have you dreaming of a tropical getaway - right in your own kitchen!

Servings: 2 Prep Time: 5 minutes | Ready Time: 5 minutes

Ingredients:
- 2 cups unsweetened pineapple juice
- 1 cup frozen pineapple
- 1 large banana
- 2 tablespoons coconut cream
- 1 tablespoon honey
- 2-3 drops coconut extract

- some extra frozen pineapple and coconut cream to serve

Instructions:
1. Place the pineapple juice, frozen pineapple, banana, coconut cream, honey, and coconut extract into a blender.
2. Blend until well combined and smooth.
3. Divide the smoothie between two glasses and top with extra frozen pineapple and coconut cream, if desired.
4. Serve and enjoy!

Nutrition information: 227 calories, 5.1g fat, 45.8g carbohydrates, 1.9g protein

25. Cranberry Fizz

Enjoy a bubbly and fruity drinks with this delicious Cranberry Fizz recipe, loaded with cranberry and ginger flavors.

Serving: 4-6 | Preparation Time: 5 minutes | Ready Time: 10 minutes

Ingredients:
- 1 (12 oz) can cranberry juice concentrate
- 2 (12 oz) cans of club soda
- 2 tablespoons of freshly grated ginger
- 2 tablespoons of honey
- 2 tablespoons of fresh lime juice

Instructions:
1. In a large pitcher, combine the cranberry juice concentrate, club soda, ginger, honey, and lime juice. Stir to combine.
2. Serve over ice and garnish with fresh cranberries and lime wedges.

Nutrition information: per serving: 229 calories, 10.4g carbohydrates, 10.4g sugar, 39mg sodium, 0.2g fat, 0.0g saturated fat, 0.4g protein.

26. Chocolate Mocha Freeze

Enjoy a delicious frozen treat with this Chocolate Mocha Freeze! Made with a blend of coffee, cocoa, and vanilla ice cream, this easy and tasty treat is the perfect pick-me-up.

Serving: Makes 1 large serving | Preparation Time: 5 minutes | Ready Time: 10 minutes

Ingredients:
- 1/2 cup brewed coffee
- 1/4 cup cocoa powder
- 2/3 cup vanilla ice cream
- Whipped cream for topping

Instructions:
1. In a blender, combine the brewed coffee, cocoa powder, and vanilla ice cream.
2. Blend until smooth.
3. Pour the mixture into a bowl or cup and top with whipped cream.
4. Serve and enjoy!

Nutrition information:
Calories - 435,
Fat - 16g,
Carbs - 57g,
Protein - 7.5g

27. Strawberry Shortcake

Enjoy this classic dessert of moist and fluffy cake filled with fresh strawberries and sweetened cream. Perfect for spring and summer, this Strawberry Shortcake is sure to be a hit at any gathering!

Serving: 8-10 | Preparation Time: 30 minutes | Ready Time: 1 hour

Ingredients:
- 1 package of yellow cake mix

- 2 tubs of whipped topping
- 1/2 cup sugar
- 2 pints of fresh strawberries, diced

Instructions:
1. Preheat oven to 350 degrees.
2. Prepare the cake mix according to the instructions on the package and bake a 9-inch round cake.
3. Once the cake has cooled, cut it in half, forming two 9-inch rounds.
4. In a medium bowl, combine the whipped topping, sugar and diced strawberries.
5. Place one 9-inch round of cake on a platter and cover with the strawberry-whipped topping mixture.
6. Place the second cake round atop the first, and then top with remaining whipped topping mixture.
7. Refrigerate for at least an hour, or until chilled and ready to serve.

Nutrition information (per serving):
Calories: 202 kcal
Carbohydrate: 38g
Protein: 4g
Fat: 4g
Fiber: 4g
Sugar: 14g

28. Peachy Citrus Surprise

Peachy Citrus Surprise is a delicious, tropical-inspired dessert that combines sweet peaches and oranges with tangy limes and a creamy cream cheese custard. This delightful treat is sure to be a hit at any gathering or family dinner.

Serving: 10-12 | Preparation Time: 15 minutes | Ready Time: 1 hour

Ingredients:
- 2 cans (14 0z/396 g) of sliced peaches, in syrup
- 2 oranges, peeled and sliced
- 2 limes, peeled and sliced

- 1/2 cup (125 mL) of white sugar
- 1/4 cup (60 mL) of freshly squeezed orange juice
- 4 eggs
- 1/4 cup (60 mL) of all-purpose flour
- 2 tablespoons (30 mL) of butter, melted
- 1/2 teaspoon (2 mL) of almond extract
- 1/4 teaspoon (1 mL) of ground cinnamon
- 1 8-oz (227g) package of cream cheese

Instructions:
1. Preheat the oven to 350F (177°C). Grease a 9x13 inch baking dish.
2. In a large bowl, combine the peaches, oranges, limes, and sugar. Pour the orange juice over the mixture. Stir until the sugar has melted.
3. In a separate bowl, whisk together the eggs, flour, melted butter, almond extract, and cinnamon. Pour this mixture over the peach mixture and stir until combined.
4. Pour the entire mixture into the prepared baking dish.
5. In a small bowl, beat the cream cheese until smooth. Spread the cream cheese over the top of the peach mixture in the baking dish.
6. Bake for 45-50 minutes or until a toothpick inserted comes out clean. Let cool for 10 minutes before serving.

Nutrition information (per serving):
Calories 294
Fat 12g
Cholesterol 90mg
Sodium 114mg
Carbohydrates 44g
Fiber 3g
Protein 5g

29. Island Breeze

Island Breeze is a refreshing tropical drink made of tropical fruits, lemon and lime juices, and coconut flavored rum. This cool and flavorful beverage will whisk you away to your own tropical paradise.

Serving: 4| Preparation Time: 5 minutes| Ready Time: 5 minutes

Ingredients:
- 1 coconut rum
- 1/2 cup pineapple juice
- 1/4 cup orange juice
- 2 tablespoons lime juice
- 2 tablespoons lemon juice
- 1 tablespoon granulated sugar (optional, to taste)
- 2 tablespoons coconut flakes

Instructions:
1. In a shaker, add all the ingredients except the coconut flakes.
2. Shake well and pour the mixture into 4 glasses.
3. Garnish with the coconut flakes.

Nutrition information: Per serving, Island Breeze contains 204 calories, 0.9 g fat, 12g sugar, 0.3g fat and 38 mg of sodium.

30. Pomegranate Lemonade

Enjoy a refreshingly tart twist on your favorite summer beverage with this easy and delicious Pomegranate Lemonade.

Serving: 4-6 | Preparation Time: 15-20 minutes | Ready Time: 1-2 hours

Ingredients:
- 1 cup of pomegranate juice
- 1/2 cup of freshly squeezed lemon juice
- 1/2 cup of sugar
- 4 cups of water
- Ice cubes as desired

Instructions:
1. In a large bowl, mix together the pomegranate juice, lemon juice and sugar.
2. Add in the water and mix everything together well.
3. Taste and adjust the sweetness of the mixture according to your preference.

4. Pour the mixture into a pitcher and let it chill for 1-2 hours in the refrigerator.
5. Before serving, add some ice cubes and make any adjustments to the sweetness, if necessary.
6. Serve and enjoy!

Nutrition information (per serving):
Calories: 125
Total Fat: 0g
Saturated Fat: 0g
Cholesterol: 0mg
Sodium: 1mg
Carbohydrates: 33g
Fiber: 0g
Sugar: 27g
Protein: 0g

31. Cranberry Sipper

Cranberry Sipper – A deliciously sweet and tart drink perfect for sipping on a warm summer day.

Serving: 4 | Preparation Time: 5 minutes | Ready Time: 5 minutes

Ingredients:
- 1 cup of fresh cranberry juice
- 2/3 cup of sparkling water
- 1/2 cup of freshly squeezed orange juice
- 4 tablespoons of freshly squeezed lime juice
- 4 tablespoons of simple syrup

Instructions:
1. Combine the cranberry juice, sparkling water, orange juice, lime juice, and simple syrup together in a large pitcher.
2. Stir until all of the ingredients are mixed together.
3. Pour the sipper into four individual glasses over ice.
4. Garnish with a wedge of lime, if desired.

Nutrition information (per serving): 90 Calories, 0 g fat, 0 mg cholesterol, 5 g carbohydrates, 9 g sugar, 0 g protein

32. Apricot Sunrise

Apricot Sunrise is a delicious and creamy vegan smoothie that combines fresh apricots, pineapple, coconut cream, banana, and dates for a sweet and refreshing treat.

Serving: 2-3 | Preparation Time: 10 minutes | Ready Time: 10 minutes

Ingredients:
- 2 cups fresh apricots
- 1 cup pineapple
- 1 cup coconut cream
- 1 banana
- 2-3 pitted dates

Instructions:
1. Peel the apricots and cut each one into four pieces
2. Place the apricots, pineapple, coconut cream, banana and dates into a blender
3. Blend until smooth
4. Pour into two to three glasses and serve

Nutrition information:
Calories: 230 kcal, Total Fat: 11 g, Saturated Fat: 9 g, Potassium: 576 mg, Carbohydrates: 33 g, Protein: 4 g, Sodium: 7 mg, Fiber: 5 g.

33. Kiwi Mojito

Kiwi Mojito is a light and refreshing cocktail with the sweet and tart flavor of kiwi. The perfect drink for any summer day!

Serving: 2 | Preparation Time: 5 minutes | Ready Time: 5 minutes

Ingredients:

- 2 kiwis, peeled and sliced
- 2 ounces sugar syrup
- 2 limes, juice and zest (or 6 ounces lime juice)
- 4 ounces white rum
- 4 ounces club soda
- Ice
- Fresh mint, for garnish

Instructions:
1. In a highball glass, muddle the kiwis to release their flavor.
2. Add the sugar syrup and lime juice.
3. Add rum to the glass and stir.
4. Fill the glass with ice and club soda.
5. Garnish with mint sprigs and a slice of lime.

Nutrition information: 133 calories per serving, 0g fat, 0g cholesterol, 11g carbohydrates, 1g protein.

34. Cucumber Mint Fizz

Beat the summer heat with this refreshing and light cocktail - the Cucumber Mint Fizz. The unique and flavourful blend of cucumber and mint is complemented nicely with the addition of club soda, giving it an ice-cold, bubbly kick.

Serving: 1 cocktail | Preparation Time: 5 minutes | Ready Time: 5 minutes

Ingredients:
- 2 ounces gin
- 2 slices cucumber
- 3-4 fresh mint leaves
- 1/2 lemon, juiced
- 2 teaspoons simple syrup
- 2 ounces of club soda

Instructions:

1. In a cocktail shaker, combine gin, cucumber slices, mint leaves and lemon juice.
2. Muddle the cucumber, mint, and lemon juice together until they are thoroughly crushed.
3. Add simple syrup to the mix and fill shaker with ice.
4. Shake vigorously for about 15 seconds.
5. Strain mixture into a glass filled with ice, and top with club soda.
6. Garnish with a couple of slices of cucumber and mint leaves.

Nutrition information: Per serving: Calories: 168, Total fat: 0g, Saturated fat: 0g, Cholesterol: 0mg, Sodium: 105mg, Total carbohydrates: 11g, Sugars: 4g, Protein: 0g.

35. Tropical Dream

Tropical Dream is a quick and easy summer-inspired dessert made with a combination of pineapple, bananas, kiwi, and other tropical fruits. With its light and refreshing flavor, this simple sweet treat is perfect for any occasion.

Serving: 4-6 | Preparation Time: 10 minutes | Ready Time: 20 minutes

Ingredients:
- 2 bananas, sliced
- 2 cups pineapple, diced
- 1 cup kiwi, diced
- 2 tablespoons shredded coconut
- 1/4 cup lime juice
- 2 tablespoons honey

Instructions:
1. In a medium bowl, mix together the pineapple, kiwi and banana slices.
2. In a small bowl, whisk together the coconut, lime juice and honey.
3. Pour the mixture over the fruit and mix until combined.
4. Place the fruit mixture in a serving dish and chill for at least 15 minutes before serving.

Nutrition information:

Calories: 109; Total Fat: 2g; Saturated Fat: 1g; Cholesterol: 0mg; Sodium: 5mg; Total Carbohydrates: 25g; Fiber: 4g; Sugar: 16g; Protein: 1g.

36. Lemon Meringue Freeze

Lemon Meringue Freeze is a light and refreshing summer treat that is perfect for any occasion. A creamy blend of lemon sorbet, whipped cream and meringue makes for a delicious combination!

Serving: 8-10 | Preparation Time: 15 minutes

Ingredients:
- 2 1/2 cups lemon sorbet, softened
- 2/3 cup heavy whipping cream
- 1/3 cup sugar
- 4 large egg whites
- 1/4 teaspoon cream of tartar

Instructions:
1. In a large bowl, fold together the lemon sorbet and heavy cream until well combined.
2. In another bowl, beat the egg whites until they form stiff peaks, then fold in the sugar and cream of tartar.
3. Once the egg whites are lightly combined, transfer them to the lemon mix and fold until just combined.
4. Use an ice cream scoop to transfer the mix into individual ramekins.
5. Cover the ramekins and place them in the freezer for at least 2 hours before serving.
6. Serve with a dollop of whipped cream, if desired.

Nutrition information: calories = 130, fat = 6g, protein = 2g, carbohydrates = 18g, sodium = 5mg

37. Honeydew Breeze

Honeydew Breeze is a refreshing and revitalizing drink perfect for those hot summer days. This beverage is a light and fruity blend of honeydew, lemon and mint and comes together quickly for an easy and delicious treat.

Serving: 4 | Preparation Time: 10 minutes | Ready Time: 10 minutes

Ingredients:
- 2 cups of honeydew, cubed
- 2 tablespoons of lemon juice
- 1/4 cup of fresh mint leaves
- 1/4 cup of honey
- 1/4 cup of ice cubes
- 2 cups of cold water

Instructions:
1. In a blender, combine cubed honeydew, lemon juice, mint leaves and honey. Blend until smooth.
2. Add the ice cubes and cold water and blend for one additional minute.
3. Pour honeydew breeze into glasses, garnish with mint leaves, and serve.

Nutrition information:
Serving Size: 1 cup; Calories: 90; Total Fat: 0g; Cholesterol: 0mg; Sodium: 14mg; Carbohydrate: 23.5g; Protein: 1.7g.

38. Pink Paradise

Pink Paradise is a delicious and refreshing gluten-free vegan smoothie that energizes and satisfies.

Serving: 2 | Preparation Time: 10 minutes | Ready Time: 10 minutes

Ingredients:
- 2 cups frozen strawberries
- 2 ripe bananas
- 1 cup non-dairy milk (e.g. coconut, almond, hemp)
- 1 teaspoon pure maple syrup

Instructions:

1. Place all ingredients in a blender and blend until smooth and creamy.
2. Divide the smoothie between two glasses and enjoy.

Nutrition information: Approximately 75 kcal per serving, 5g dietary fiber, 10g carbohydrate, 1g fat, 1g protein.

39. Cinnamon Punch

This Cinnamon Punch is an easy-to-make and refreshing combination of apple cider, cranberry juice and seasonal spices. With its sweet and tart flavor, it's a great choice for any winter gathering or holiday party.

Serving: 12-14 | Preparation Time: 5 minutes | Ready Time: 4 hours

Ingredients:
- 5 cups apple cider
- 2 cups cranberry juice
- 1 tablespoon cinnamon
- 1/4 teaspoon nutmeg
- 1 teaspoon allspice
- 2 cinnamon sticks

Instructions:
1. In a large bowl, combine the apple cider, cranberry juice, cinnamon, nutmeg, and allspice.
2. Stir until combined.
3. Place the cinnamon sticks in a large pitcher and pour the juice mixture over it.
4. Refrigerate for at least 4 hours or until chilled.
5. Serve over ice.

Nutrition information (per 1/2 cup):
- Calories: 60
- Protein: 0g
- Total Fat: 0g
- Carbohydrates: 16g
- Sugars: 15g
- Sodium: 5mg

- Potassium: 41mg

40. Grapefruit Zinger

Grapefruit Zinger is a refreshing and tangy breakfast or lunch meal that is both easy to prepare and sure to delight. Serve it as a light snack or as a main meal to tantalize your taste buds.

Serves 4. | Preparation Time: 10 minutes | Ready Time: 10 minutes

Ingredients:
-2 medium-sized pink grapefruits
-1/4 cup honey
-1 tablespoon freshly grated ginger
-2 tablespoons freshly squeezed lime juice
-1/4 teaspoon ground black pepper
-1/4 cup freshly chopped mint leaves

Instructions:
1. Peel and section the grapefruits, reserving the juices.
2. Combine the honey, ginger, lime juice, pepper, mint leaves and the reserved grapefruit juices in a small bowl. Mix until everything is well combined.
3. Place the grapefruit sections in a shallow bowl or plate.
4. Pour the honey mixture over the grapefruit and toss to combine.
5. Allow to sit for at least 10 minutes to let the flavors mingle.

Nutrition information: per serving: 138 calories, 0g fat, 36g carbs, 1g protein.

41. Party Punch

Party Punch is a deliciously fruity and lightly sweet drink that can be customised for any occasion. Perfect for festive gatherings, this recipe is sure to be a hit!

Serving: Makes 15 | Preparation Time: 10 minutes | Ready Time: 10 minutes

Ingredients:
- 2 cartons (2 L each) tropical juice like SunnyD
- 1 can (46 oz) pineapple juice
- 1L ginger ale
- 2L 7 Up or Sprite
- 2 cans (11 oz each) mandarin oranges, drained
- 2 cups frozen strawberries
- 2 cups frozen peaches
- 1 cup sugar

Instructions:
1. In a large punch bowl, mix tropical juice, pineapple juice, ginger ale, 7 Up or Sprite and sugar.
2. Add oranges, strawberries, and peaches to punch. Stir gently.
3. Serve immediately or store in the refrigerator until ready to serve.

Nutrition information:
Calories: 73.3 kcal, Carbohydrates: 18.3 g, Protein: 0.5 g, Fat: 0.2 g, Saturated Fat: 0 g, Cholesterol: 0 mg, Sodium: 5.1 mg, Potassium: 29.5 mg, Fiber: 0.8 g, Sugar: 15.2 g, Vitamin A: 11 IU, Vitamin C: 8.1 mg, Calcium: 14 mg, Iron: 0 mg.

42. Peachy Sunrise

"Peachy Sunrise" is a delightful and flavorful breakfast smoothie that is perfect for a morning pick-me-up. It is sweet, refreshing, and easy to make.

Serving: 1 | Preparation Time: 5 minutes

Ingredients:
-1 banana
-1/2 cup frozen peaches
-1/4 cup pineapple juice
-1/4 cup plain yogurt

-Honey, to taste

Instructions:
1. Put all ingredients in a blender and blend until smooth.
2. Taste and add honey, if desired.
3. Serve and enjoy!

Nutrition information: (per serving)
Calories: 158, Fat: 0.4g, Carbohydrates: 36g, Protein: 3.6g, Sodium: 20mg, Fiber: 2.7g

43. Sweet Tangerine Treat

Sweet Tangerine Treat is an easy to make and delicious dessert that is sure to please everyone. This citrusy treat is perfect for summertime or anytime you are craving something sweet and light.

Serving: 8 servings | Preparation Time: 20 minutes | Ready Time: 3 hours

Ingredients:
- 2 cups of white sugar
- 3 tablespoons of orange zest
- 2/3 cup of fresh- squeezed tangerine juice
- 2/3 cup of melted butter or margarine
- 2 1/2 cups of all-purpose flour
- 1/2 teaspoon of salt
- 2 teaspoons of baking soda
- 2 tablespoons of ground cinnamon
- 2 tablespoons of nutmeg
- 3 cups of sifted powdered sugar
- 1/3 cup of tangerine-flavored liqueur

Instructions:
1. Preheat oven to 350 degrees F.
2. In a medium bowl, mix together the sugar, orange zest, tangerine juice, and butter or margarine until smooth.
3. In a separate bowl, mix together flour, salt, baking soda, and spices.

4. Gradually add the dry ingredients to the wet ingredients, and mix until combined.
5. Grease a 9x13 inch baking pan, and spread the mixture evenly in the pan.
6. Bake in preheated oven for 30 minutes, or until lightly golden brown.
7. Let cool completely before frosting.
8. In a medium bowl, mix together sifted powdered sugar and tangerine-flavored liqueur until smooth.
9. Spread the frosting over the cooled cake.

Nutrition information:
Calories: 241, Fat: 5.1g, Carbohydrates: 45.3g, Protein: 2.4g, Cholesterol: 10.3mg, Sodium: 229.4mg.

44. Pina Colada Float

Refresh your taste buds with a delicious and easy-to-make Pina Colada Float! This delightful dessert mixes creamy coconut ice cream with the sweet and tangy taste of pineapple to create a perfect combination.

Serving: Makes enough for two generous servings | Preparation Time: 10 minutes | Ready Time: 10 minutes

Ingredients:
- 1/2 cup crushed pineapple
- 1/2 cup cream of coconut
- 2 cups pineapple juice
- 2 scoops coconut ice cream
- Maraschino cherries and shredded coconut (optional, for garnish)

Instruction:
1. In a medium-sized bowl, combine the crushed pineapple, cream of coconut and pineapple juice. Mix together until well blended.
2. Pour the prepared mixture into two glasses and place a scoop of coconut ice cream in each glass.
3. Garnish with maraschino cherries and shredded coconut, if desired.
4. Serve and enjoy!

Nutrition information:
Per Serving (Based on 1 Serving): Calories: 310, Carbohydrates: 43g, Protein: 1g, Fat: 16g, Saturated Fat: 12g, Cholesterol: 31mg, Sodium: 20mg, Potassium: 106mg, Fiber: 2g, Sugar: 33g, Vitamin A: 84IU, Vitamin C: 11mg, Calcium: 59mg, Iron: 1mg.

45. Mango Tango

Mango Tango is a sweet and zesty treat, bursting with flavor! This quick and easy treat is made with a combination of mango and citrus, and is perfect for hot summer days.

Serving: 4 | Preparation Time: 10 minutes | Ready Time: 25 minutes

Ingredients:
- 2 ripe mangoes, diced
- 2 cups pineapple juice
- 1/2 cup orange juice
- 3 limes, juiced
- 1 teaspoon of honey
- 1/2 teaspoon of freshly ground ginger
- Ice cubes

Instructions:
1. In a blender, blend together mango, pineapple and orange juice, lime juice, honey and ground ginger together until smooth.
2. Place ice cubes into glasses and pour blended mixture over top.
3. Serve chilled and enjoy!

Nutrition information: (Per Serving)
- Calories: 144
- Protein: 2 g
- Carbohydrates: 33 g
- Fiber: 3 g
- Total Fat: 0.1 g
- Sodium: 3 mg

46. Melon Punch

Melon Punch is a delicious, fruity drink that is great for any occasion. It is a refreshing, sweet and fruity combination of melon, mango, pineapple and lemon-lime soda sure to please everyone.

Serving: Serves 4-6 | Preparation Time: 10 minutes | Ready Time: 10 minutes

Ingredients:
- 2 cups cubed fresh watermelon
- 1 cup cubed fresh mango
- 2 cups pineapple juice
- 2 litres lemon-lime soda
- 2-3 tablespoons honey or sugar

Instructions:
1. Place watermelon, mango, and pineapple juice in a blender and blend until smooth.
2. Pour the mixture into a large pitcher or punch bowl.
3. Pour lemon-lime soda into the mixture and stir in honey or sugar to taste.
4. Serve over ice in individual glasses, or store in the refrigerator for up to 3 days.

Nutrition information: per serving: %174 Calories; 0.3g fat; 0mg cholesterol; 45.3g carbohydrates; 0g protein; 5.9mg sodium.

47. Banana Banana Shake

Banana Banana Shake is a delicious, creamy, and nutritious smoothie that is perfect for a morning pick-me-up or post workout snack. Rich and sweet, this shake will become your go-to favorite!

Serving: 2 | Preparation Time: 5 minutes | Ready Time: 5 minutes

Ingredients:
- 2 ripe bananas

- 1/4 cup low-fat milk
- 4-5 ice cubes
- 2 tablespoons honey
- 1/2 teaspoon vanilla extract

Instructions:
1. Peel and slice the bananas into a blender.
2. Add the milk, honey and vanilla extract.
3. Blend until smooth.
4. Add the ice cubes and blend until they're fully incorporated.

Nutrition information (per serving):
- Calories: 135
- Total Fat: 0 g
- Saturated Fat: 0 g
- Cholesterol: 2 mg
- Sodium: 40 mg
- Total Carbohydrate: 35 g
- Dietary Fiber: 2 g
- Sugar: 23 g
- Protein: 2 g

48. Orange Dream Swirl

Orange Dream Swirl is a delicious creamy citrus cake dessert that can be enjoyed in the summertime. It's sweet and zesty, finished with a soft orange infused cream.

This recipe serves 8 people, | takes 10 minutes to prepare, | is ready in 45 minutes.

Ingredients:
-1/2 cup butter
-1/2 cup white sugar
-2 eggs
-2 to 3 oranges, zested and juiced
-1/2 teaspoon baking powder
-1/2 teaspoon baking soda

-1/2 teaspoon salt
-2 cups all-purpose flour
-1/2 cup sour cream
-1/2 cup confectioners sugar
-8 ounces cream cheese, softened

Instructions:
1. Preheat oven to 350 degrees F
2. In a bowl, cream together the butter and sugar until light and fluffy.
3. Beat in the eggs one at a time.
4. Stir in the orange zest, juice, baking powder, baking soda, and salt.
5. Gradually stir in the flour.
6. Pour the cake batter into a 9-inch cake pan that is greased and lightly floured.
7. Bake cake in preheated oven for 30 minutes, or until a toothpick inserted in the center comes out clean.
8. Allow cake to cool in the pan for 10 minutes.
9. In a separate bowl, beat together the sour cream, confectioners sugar, and cream cheese until smooth.
10. Spread cream cheese mixture over cooled cake.
11. Cut cake into 8 pieces to serve.

Nutrition information (per serving): Calories 330, Fat 17g, Saturated Fat 10g, Cholesterol 78mg, Sodium 241mg, Carbohydrates 39g, Fiber 0.5g, Protein 5.5g

49. Apple Slammer

Apple Slammer is an aptly named smoothie that is easy to make and tastes delicious. Combining apple juice and yogurt, this fruity treat is a great way to start off the day or provide a refreshing snack on a hot summer day.

Serving: 2| Preparation Time: 5 minutes| Ready Time: 5 minutes

Ingredients:
- 1 cup of unsweetened apple juice
- 1/2 cup of plain yogurt

- 1/2 cup of frozen apple slices
- 2 tablespoons of honey

Instructions:
1. Place all of the ingredients in a blender and blend until smooth.
2. Serve your Apple Slammer in 2 glasses.

Nutrition information:
Calories- 180 calories
Fat- 1 gram
Carbohydrates- 40 grams
Protein- 6 grams

50. Strawberry Breeze

Strawberry Breeze is a cool, refreshing and tasty smoothie that is perfect for a hot summer day. This easy-to-make smoothie is made with just a few ingredients, hardly takes any time and is packed with nutrition.

Serving: 2| Preparation Time: 5 mins | Ready Time: 5 mins

Ingredients:
- 3/4 cup unsweetened almond milk
- 1/2 cup frozen strawberries
- 1 banana
- 5 ice cubes
- 1 teaspoon of honey

Instructions:
1. Place all the ingredients into a high-speed blender.
2. Blend the ingredients until smooth.
3. Pour into two glasses and enjoy.

Nutrition information (per serving):
- Calories: 127
- Carbs: 30 g
- Protein: 2 g
- Fat: 2 g

51. Cherry Limeade

This refreshing cherry limeade is the perfect summer drink to cool off on a hot day. It is easy to make and only requires a few ingredients.

Serving: 4 | Preparation Time: 10 minutes | Ready Time: 10 minutes

Ingredients:
- 1 cup freshly squeezed lime juice
- 3/4 cup of cold water
- 1/2 cup of cherry syrup
- 1/4 cup of sugar
- 4-6 cups of ice

Instructions:
1. In a large bowl, combine the lime juice, water, cherry syrup, and sugar and whisk them together until combined.
2. Place the ice in individual glasses and then distribute the limeade among them.
3. Serve cold with a slice of lime, if desired.

Nutrition information:
Calories: 127; Total Fat: 0 g; Cholesterol: 0 mg; Sodium: 11 mg; Total Carbohydrates: 33 g; Protein: 0 g; Fiber: 0 g.

52. Raspberry Sunrise

Raspberry Sunrise is a beautiful and delicious smoothie that's filled with fiber and nutrition. Its sweet and tangy raspberry flavor is the perfect way to start your morning.

Serving: Makes 2 servings| Preparation Time: 5 minutes| Ready Time: 5 minutes

Ingredients:
- 1 cup frozen raspberries

- 1 banana
- 1/2 cup almond milk
- 1/2 cup greek yogurt
- 2 tablespoons honey

Instructions:
1. Add the frozen raspberries, banana, almond milk, yogurt, and honey into a blender.
2. Blend the ingredients until a smooth consistency is achieved.
3. Divide the smoothie between two glasses and enjoy.

Nutrition information (per serving):
Calories: 226 kcal
Carbohydrates: 36.5 g
Fiber: 4.5 g
Sugar: 25.8 g
Protein: 4.9 g
Fat: 5.8 g

53. Tutti Frutti Twist

Tutti Frutti Twist is a delicious and refreshing summer pastry that combines sliced fruits and fluffy, bright cream cheese whipped cream frosting. This dessert is the perfect way to cool down in the summer months and is surprisingly easy to make.

Serving: 8| Preparation Time: 10 minutes| Ready Time: 30 minutes

Ingredients:
- 2 cups all-purpose flour
- 1 cup granulated sugar
- 1 teaspoon baking powder
- 1 teaspoon baking soda
- 1 cup butter, softened
- 3 eggs
- 1 teaspoon vanilla extract
- 2 tablespoons fresh lemon juice

- 1 cup chopped fresh or canned fruit of your choice (strawberries, raspberries, peaches, etc.)
For the Frosting:
- 8 oz. cream cheese, softened
- 1 stick butter, softened
- 2-3 cups confectioner's sugar
- 1 teaspoon vanilla extract

Instructions
1. Preheat oven to 350F and grease a 9x13" baking pan.
2. In a medium bowl, whisk together the flour, sugar, baking powder, and baking soda.
3. In the bowl of an electric mixer, cream together the butter, eggs, and vanilla until light and fluffy. Then, slowly add in the flour mixture, mixing until just combined.
4. Pour the batter into the prepared baking pan and spread evenly.
5. Top the batter with the chopped fruit of your choice.
6. Bake in the preheated oven for 25-30 minutes, until a tester inserted in the center comes out clean.
7. Meanwhile, in the bowl of an electric mixer, cream together the cream cheese, butter, confectioner's sugar, and vanilla until light and fluffy.
8. Spread the frosting over the cooled cake and sprinkle with more chopped fruit.

Nutrition information:
Calories: 298kcal, Carbohydrates: 32g, Protein: 4g, Fat: 17g, Saturated Fat: 10g, Cholesterol: 86mg, Sodium: 179mg, Potassium: 73mg, Fiber: 1g, Sugar: 19g, Vitamin A: 837IU, Vitamin C: 1mg, Calcium: 61mg, Iron: 1mg

54. Mocktail Margarita

Mocktail Margarita is a festive and easy-to-make non-alcoholic version of the classic Margarita cocktail. This delicious drink is perfect for any celebration, with a zesty and refreshing combination of tart lime and sweet orange.

Serving: 8 | Preparation Time: 10 minutes | Ready Time: 10 minutes

Ingredients:
- 1 (32-ounce) bottle lemon-lime soda
- 2 cups orange juice
- Juice from 2 limes
- 1/4 cup sugar
- 2 tablespoons agave nectar

Instruction:
1. In a large pitcher, mix together the soda, orange juice, lime juice, sugar, and agave nectar.
2. Serve over ice and garnish with orange and lime slices.

Nutrition Facts:
Per Serving: 75 calories, 0.2g fat, 18.2g carbohydrates, 12.2g sugar, 0.3g protein

55. Blueberry Limeade

Blueberry Limeade is a refreshing, tangy and sweet summer drink perfect for an afternoon barbecue or relaxing summer day. It's simple to make, and is the perfect blend of tart limeade and juicy blueberry sweetness.

Servings: 4 | Preparation Time: 10 minutes | Ready Time: 10 minutes

Ingredients:
- 4 cups cold water
- 4 limes, juiced
- 1/2 cup granulated sugar
- 1/2 cup frozen blueberries

Instructions:
1. In a large pitcher, mix together the water, lime juice and sugar. Stir until the sugar is dissolved.
2. Add the blueberries and mash with a wooden spoon adding more water if desired for a thinner consistency.
3. Stir to combine and let sit for 5 minutes.
4. Serve over ice with a lime wedge.

Nutrition information:
Serving size: 8 ounces
Calories: 116
Total fat: 0 g
Cholesterol: 0 mg
Sodium: 1 mg
Total Carbs: 29 g
Protein: 0 g

56. Pear Sorbet Float

This refreshing Pear Sorbet Float is the perfect way to cool off on a hot summer day! Using just 8 simple ingredients, it is easy to make and nutritious!

Serves 4. | Preparation Time: 10 minutes. | Ready in 10 minutes.

Ingredients:
- 4 cups of pear sorbet
- 4 cups of plain seltzer
- 4 tablespoons of honey
- 4 tablespoons of fresh squeezed lemon juice
- 1 tablespoons of lemon zest
- 1 teaspoon of almond extract
- 4 slices of fresh pear
- Mint for garnish

Instructions:
1. Place two scoops of pear sorbet into each of the four serving glasses.
2. Top each glass with a cup of seltzer and stir lightly with a spoon.
3. In a bowl, mix the honey, lemon juice, lemon zest, and almond extract together until combined.
4. Drizzle the mixture over each glass of seltzer and pear sorbet.
5. Place a pear slice in each glass.
6. Garnish with a sprig of mint and serve immediately.

Nutrition information:

Calories: 200
Fat: 5g
Carbs: 35g
Protein: 2g

57. Peachy Green Cooler

This refreshing Peachy Green Cooler is packed with flavor and great nutrition, thanks to the combination of cucumbers and peaches. Perfect summertime drink to cool off with, it is extremely easy to make and comes together in no time.

Serving: 4| Preparation Time: 5 minutes| Ready Time: 5 minutes

Ingredients:
- 2 cups fresh or frozen peaches
- 1 English cucumber, peeled and chopped
- 1/2 cup fresh mint leaves
- 1/4 cup honey
- 4 cups water
- Ice cubes

Instructions:
1. Place peaches, cucumber, mint leaves, honey and 2 cups of water in a blender and blend until smooth.
2. Add remaining 2 cups water and blend until completely mixed.
3. Pour the mixture into glasses over ice cubes.
4. Garnish with fresh mint leaves, if desired.

Nutrition information: Per one serving (1 cup); Calories 120, Fat 0g, Cholesterol 0mg, Sodium 0mg, Carbohydrate 32g, Fiber 3g, Sugar 25g, Protein 1g.

58. Raspberry Fizz

Raspberry Fizz is an easy to make, bubbly and refreshing drink perfect for a summer day. Serve this delicious drink to family and friends for a special refreshment.

Serving: 4 | Preparation Time: 10 minutes | Ready Time: 10 minutes

Ingredients:
- 2 cups of crushed ice
- 1 cup of raspberry juice
- 1/2 cup of lemon-lime soda
- 2 tablespoons of honey
- 2 tablespoons of granulated sugar
- Optional: 6 to 7 mint leaves

Instructions:
1. In a blender, combine crushed ice, raspberry juice, lemon-lime soda, honey, and sugar. Blend until ingredients are completely mixed together.
2. For an added flavor, add in 6 to 7 mint leaves, then blend for about 10 to 15 more seconds.
3. Pour the Raspberry Fizz over a glass filled with crushed ice. Add a few more mint leaves for garnishing, if desired.

Nutrition information:
Per serving, this recipe has approximately 144 calories, 0 g total fat, 37 g total carbohydrate, 0 g protein, 18 mg sodium, and 0 g dietary fiber.

59. Elderflower Freeze

This refreshing and flavorful Elderflower Freeze is sure to be a hit with family and friends. An icy and sweet beverage, this drink is perfect for summer barbecues or evenings on the patio.

Serving: 6 | Prep Time: 5 mins

Ingredients:
- 2 cups of elderflower cordial
- 2 liters of carbonated lemon-lime soda
- 3 tablespoons of fresh lemon juice

- 1 liter of orange juice
- 1/2 cup of sugar

Instructions:
1. In a pitcher, combine elderflower cordial, carbonated lemon-lime soda, lemon juice, orange juice, and sugar. Stir until the sugar is dissolved.
2. Divide the Elderflower Freeze into glasses filled with ice and garnish with orange slices or fresh mint leaves.

Nutrition information:
Calories: 178, Fat: 0g, Carbs: 46g, Protein: 0g

60. Passion Fruit Frappe

This delicious Passion Fruit Frappe is a quick and easy summer drink! It makes a great refreshing and cooling beverage to enjoy on a hot day.

Serves: 4 people, | Preparation Time: 15 minutes, | Ready Time: 15 minutes,

Ingredients:
- 2 1/2 cups cold passion fruit juice,
- 2 tablespoons caster sugar,
- 4 tablespoons of black tea (taken from 4 teabags),
- 1 cup of crushed ice,
- 1 cup of cold full-cream milk,
- 1 teaspoon of fresh lemon juice and optional mint leaves for garnish.

Instructions:
1. In a blender, combine the cold passion fruit juice and sugar and blend until the sugar is dissolved.
2. Add the black tea and blend until blended. Add the crushed ice, milk and lemon juice and blend until all of the ingredients are evenly blended, 2–3 minutes.
3. Pour the drink into 4 glasses and add a few mint leaves, if desired.

Nutritional Information: Per serving (1 cup): Calories 137, Fat 2g, Cholesterol 6mg, Sodium 60mg, Carbohydrate 28g, Fiber 0.5g, Protein 3g.

61. Orange Crush

Orange Crush is a delicious, refreshing drink that is easy to make and has a unique sweet-tart taste. It's made with freshly squeezed oranges, tangy orange soda, and a hint of lemon and lime. This is sure to be a crowd-pleaser for any occasion!

Serving: 6 | Preparation Time: 10 minutes | Ready Time: 10 minutes

Ingredients:
- 6 freshly squeezed oranges
- 1 liter of chilled orange soda
- 2 limes, freshly squeezed
- 2 lemons, freshly squeezed
- Ice

Instructions:
1. Squeeze the oranges, limes, and lemons into a pitcher.
2. Pour in the chilled orange soda.
3. Add a few cups of ice and stir to combine.
4. Serve in the glasses and garnish with slices of oranges, limes, or lemons.

Nutrition information:
Calories: 250
Total Fat: 0 g
Saturated Fat: 0 g
Cholesterol: 0 mg
Sodium: 20 mg
Total Carbohydrates: 27 g
Fiber: 2.5 g
Sugar: 22 g
Protein: 1.5 g

62. Mojito Popsicle

Mojito Popsicles are a refreshing and delicious treat that can be enjoyed on a hot summer day. These popsicles are easy to make and only require a few simple ingredients. Serve up to 5 people and they can be ready in 5 hours.

Serving: 5 people| Preparation Time: 10 minutes | Ready Time: 5 hours

Ingredients:
- 1 cup white sugar
- 6 mint leaves
- 1 cup cream of coconut
- 1 cup lime juice
- 1 liter club soda
- 20-25 popsicle molds

Instructions:
1. In a blender, blend together the sugar, mint leaves and coconut cream until a thick paste has formed.
2. Add the lime juice and club soda and blend for a few seconds until combined.
3. Fill the popsicle molds with the mixture and freeze for 5 hours or until completely solid.
4. Enjoy your Mojito Popsicles!

Nutrition information: Per serving 1 popsicle, Cal 188, Total Fat 4.4g, Sodium 91mg, Total Carbohydrates 37.7g, Protein 0.9g.

63. Peach Breeze

Peach Breeze is a delicious fruit smoothie, perfect for a hot summer day. It's a light, refreshing blend of sweet and tart flavors, with a unique punch of peach.

Serving: 2 | Preparation Time: 5 minutes | Ready Time: 5 minutes

Ingredients:
- 1 cup diced peaches
- 1 ripe banana
- 1/3 cup orange juice
- 1/3 cup pineapple juice
- 4-5 ice cubes

Instructions:
1. Place the diced peaches and banana in a blender.
2. Pour in the orange and pineapple juices, and add ice cubes.
3. Blend until the mixture is smooth.
4. Serve in glasses with a garnish of peach slices, if desired.

Nutrition information:
Calories: 112; Total Fat: 0 g; Cholesterol: 0 mg; Sodium: 16 mg; Total Carbohydrate: 28 g; Dietary Fiber: 2 g; Protein: 1 g; Vitamin A: 4%; Vitamin C: 58%; Calcium: 1%; Iron: 2%.

64. Mango Margarita

Bright and sunny, Mango Margaritas are a delicious, slightly exotic take on the traditional favorite. Perfect for happy hour or day or evening by the pool, this summery drink is made with sweet mango puree, margarita mix and silver tequila.

Serving: Serves 4| Preparation Time: 5 minutes| Ready Time: 5 minutes

Ingredients:
-3 cups frozen mango
-2 cups margarita mix
-1 1/2 cups silver tequila
-Ice, for serving
-Kosher salt, for rimming glasses
-Lime wedges, for garnish

Instruction:
1. Put the frozen mango in a blender, along with the margarita mix and tequila.

2. Blend until the margarita is the desired consistency.
3. Use a lime wedge, and run it around the rim of a margarita glass. Dip the glass in a plate of kosher salt.
4. Divide the blended mango margarita between the prepared glasses and serve with ice.
5. Garnish with a lime wedge and serve immediately.

Nutrition information: (per serving)
-Calories: 250
-Total Fat: 0g
-Saturated Fat: 0g
-Cholesterol: 0mg
-Sodium: 110mg
-Total Carbolhydrates: 28g
-Dietary Fiber: 0g
-Protein: 0g

65. Strawberry Cream Soda

If you are looking for a sweet and fruity beverage, then homemade strawberry cream soda will be the perfect treat! This recipe serves four and only takes 10 minutes of | Preparation Time, with a ready time of 10 minutes. With a little bit of effort, you can make a delicious concoction of strawberries and cream soda pop.

Serving- 4| Preparation Time- 10 minutes | Ready Time- 10 minutes

Ingredients-
- 4 cups of cream soda
- 2 cups of frozen or fresh strawberries
- 2 tablespoons of honey
- 3 tablespoons of fresh lemon juice
- 1/4 cup of heavy cream
- 2 tablespoons of sugar
- Sprinkles and maraschino cherries, optional

Instructions-

1. In a blender, combine cream soda, honey, fresh lemon juice and fresh or frozen strawberries. Blend until the mixture is smooth.
2. Pour the mixture into four glasses and top with heavy cream, sugar and ice cubes.
3. Garnish with sprinkles and/or maraschino cherries, if desired.

Nutrition information-
Calories- 253 kcal
Carbs- 47 g
Fat- 6 g
Protein- 2 g

66. Banana Sunrise

Banana Sunrise is a delicious smoothie that is made with a combination of bananas, orange juice, and mango. It's a great way to start the day off with a nutritious and refreshing breakfast.

Serving: 2| Preparation Time: 5 minutes| Ready Time: 5 minutes

Ingredients:
- 2 Bananas
- 1/2 cup Orange Juice
- 1/2 cup Mango, frozen

Instructions:
1. Peel and cut the bananas into slices.
2. Place the banana slices, orange juice, and mango into a blender.
3. Blend for about 2 minutes, until creamy.
4. Pour the smoothie into two glasses.

Nutrition information:
Calories: 178, Carbohydrates: 45g, Sugar: 28g, Sodium: 2mg, Potassium: 534mg, Vitamin A: 8%, Vitamin C: 72%, Calcium: 2%, Iron: 4%.

67. Blueberry Blast

Blueberry Blast is an easy-to-make smoothie bowl that's perfect for a quick snack or breakfast. With its delicious combination of antioxidant-rich blueberries and creamy Greek yogurt, this refreshing smoothie bowl will have your taste buds ready for more!

Serving: 1 | Preparation Time: 5 minutes | Ready Time: 5 minutes

Ingredients:
-1/2 cup frozen blueberries
-1/2 cup plain Greek yogurt
-1 tablespoon honey
-1/4 teaspoon vanilla extract
-1/2 tablespoons chia seeds
-1 teaspoon hemp hearts

Instructions:
1. In a blender, combine frozen blueberries, Greek yogurt, honey, and vanilla extract.
2. Blend until smooth.
3. Pour the smoothie in a bowl and top with chia seeds and hemp hearts.
4. Enjoy!

Nutrition information (per serving):
Calories – 127
Fat – 2.5 g
Carbohydrates – 18.5 g
Protein – 7.3 g

68. Apple and Cranberry Cooler

This delicious Apple and Cranberry Cooler is an easy-to-make and refreshing summertime beverage.

Serving: 2-3 | Preparation Time: 5 minutes | Ready Time: 10 minutes

Ingredients:
-1 cup of fresh apples, thinly sliced
-1/2 cup of fresh cranberries

-1/2 cup of orange juice
-1 cup of cold sparkling water
-Ice cubes, as desired

Instructions:
1. In a large pitcher or glass, combine the apples and cranberries.
2. Pour in the orange juice, stirring to combine.
3. Add the cold sparkling water and stir until combined.
4. Add desired amount of ice cubes.
5. Serve chilled and enjoy!

Nutrition information:
Each serving of Apple and Cranberry Cooler contains approximately 154 calories, 0g of fat, 37g of carbohydrates, 3g of protein, and 1g of fiber.

69. Mock Mai Tai

Mock Mai Tai, a tropical, nonalcoholic drink, is a great way to enjoy the classic flavors of a mai tai without the alcohol. This beverage has the tart and sweet taste of passion fruit, orange, and pineapple that the classic cocktail offers.

Servings: 4 | Preparation Time: 5 minutes | Ready Time: 5 minutes

Ingredients:
- 1 cup pineapple juice
- 1/2 cup orange juice
- 1/4 cup passion fruit juice
- Lime wedges

Instructions:
1. In a pitcher, mix together pineapple juice, orange juice and passion fruit juice.
2. Pour equal amounts of the juice mixture into four glasses.
3. Garnish each glass with a lime wedge.

Nutrition information (per serving):

Calories: 73, Total Fat: 0g, Saturated Fat: 0g, Cholesterol: 0mg, Sodium: 5mg, Carbohydrate: 18g, Fiber: 0.5g, Sugar: 15g, Protein: 0.5g

70. Orange Grapefruit Punch

This delicious Orange Grapefruit Punch is the perfect combination of flavors. Tart and sweet, this easy to make punch can be put together in minutes and perfect for serving a crowd.

Serving: 12-14 | Preparation Time: 5 minutes | Ready Time: 10 minutes

Ingredients:
- 4 cups orange juice
- 2 cups limeade, frozen or freshly made
- 1 cup all-fruit grapefruit
- 1 liter lemon soda, chilled
- 1/2 cup of white sugar

Instructions:
1. Combine the orange juice and limeade in a large pitcher or punch bowl.
2. Add in the grapefruit and stir until combined
3. Add in the lemon soda and the white sugar and mix until completely combined.
4. Serve with plenty of ice.

Nutrition information:
Serving size: 1/2 cup
Calories: 70
Total Fat: 0g
Carbohydrates: 16g
Protein: 1g

71. Melon Splash

Melon Splash is a light and refreshing summer treat that combines the sweetness of cantaloupe and honeydew melon with lime juice, honey, and mint. Not only is it incredibly easy to make, but it's also incredibly nutritious!

Serving: Serves 3 | Preparation Time: 10 minutes | Ready Time: 30 minutes

Ingredients:
- 2 cups of diced cantaloupe
- 2 cups of diced honeydew melon
- 3 tablespoons of lime juice
- 2 tablespoons of honey
- 8-10 mint leaves
- Ice cubes

Instructions:
1. In a medium-sized bowl, combine the cantaloupe, honeydew melon, lime juice, and honey.
2. Mash the mint leaves in a mortar and pestle and add them to the melon mixture.
3. Mix all the ingredients together and let stand for 10 minutes.
4. After 10 minutes, add the ice cubes to the mixture and stir until well blended.
5. Serve immediately.

Nutrition information: Per Serving: Calories: 86, Fat: 0.5 grams, Sodium: 4 milligrams, Carbohydrates: 22.5 grams, Fiber: 1.8 grams, Protein: 1.2 grams

72. Creamy Coconut Float

Creamy Coconut Float: This creamy and delicious float is the perfect summer treat. Refreshingly cool and easy to make, it's sure to hit the spot on warm days.

Serving Size: 1 float| Preparation Time: 5 minutes| Ready Time: 5 minutes

Ingredients:

- 1 scoop of vanilla ice cream
- 1/4 cup coconut cream
- 2 ounces of pineapple juice
- Whipped cream
- Maraschino cherries

Instructions:
1. Place a scoop of ice cream in a tall glass.
2. Pour coconut cream and pineapple juice over the ice cream and stir gently.
3. Top with a dollop of whipped cream and top with a cherry.

Nutrition information: Calories 130, Fat 9.9g, Carbs 7.1g, Protein 0.6g

73. Honeydew Lemonade

This refreshing Honeydew Lemonade is the perfect summer drink- sweet, with a tart kick! This cold, fruity beverage is sure to go quickly, so get ready to make a batch!

Serving: 1/2 gallon/ 8 servings | Preparation Time: 5-10 minutes | Ready Time: 5-10 minutes

Ingredients:
-3 cups of lemon juice
-1/2 cup of honey
-4 cups of cubed honeydew melon
-4-5 cups of iced water

Instructions:
1. Combine the lemon juice and honey in a pitcher, stirring until honey is dissolved.
2. Add honeydew melon and muddle until liquid is cloudy and pulp is released.
3. Add the iced water and stir.
4. Pour the mixture through a strainer over a large bowl.
5. Discard solids and pour liquid back into the pitcher.
6. Serve chilled, over ice with lemon slices, if desired.

Nutrition information:
-Calories: 70
-Fat: 0 g
-Carbohydrates: 18 g
-Protein: 1 g

74. Blueberry Mojito

Refreshing and sweet, a Blueberry Mojito is a delicious twist on a traditional classic. The combination of fresh blueberries, lime and mint is perfect for those hot summer days!

Serving: Makes 1 drink | Preparation Time: 5 minutes | Ready Time: 5 minutes

Ingredients:
-2 ounces white rum
-2 teaspoons sugar
-1/4 cup fresh blueberries
- juice from 1 lime
- 4 mint leaves
- 4 ounces club soda

Instructions:
1. In a cocktail shaker, muddle together the lime juice, sugar, mint leaves and blueberries.
2. Add the rum to the shaker and fill with ice. Shake well.
3. Strain into a glass with ice and top with club soda.
4. Garnish with more mint and a lime wedge, if desired.

Nutrition information:
Calories: 161, Total Fat: 0.1g, Cholesterol: 0mg, Sodium: 8mg, Total Carbohydrate: 11.6g, Protein: 0.7g.

75. Ginger Honey Cooler

Ginger Honey Cooler: This refreshing ginger-honey cooler is a great way to quench your thirst when the temperature rises.

Serving: 4 | Preparation Time: 10 minutes | Ready Time: 10 minutes

Ingredients:
- 8 cups cold water
- 1/2 inch fresh ginger root, diced
- 4 tablespoons honey
- 2 tablespoons lemon juice
- 1/4 teaspoon kosher or sea salt

Instructions:
1. In a large pitcher, combine the water, diced ginger, honey, lemon juice, and salt. Stir until all ingredients are well incorporated.
2. Chill in the refrigerator for 30 minutes.
3. Serve the Ginger Honey Cooler over ice and enjoy!

Nutrition information:
Calories: 30; Total Fat: 0g; Sodium: 62.5mg; Carbohydrates: 7.7g; Protein: 0g; Sugar: 6.4g.

76. Pineapple Breeze

Pineapple Breeze is a refreshing and light beverage perfect for summer days.

Serving: 4-6 | Preparation Time: 10 minutes | Ready Time: 10 minutes

Ingredients:
- 2 cups fresh or frozen pineapple
- 1 cup of water
- 2 tablespoons of honey
- 1 lime (juiced)
- 1/4 teaspoon of ground ginger

Instructions:
1. Place the pineapple, water, honey, lime juice, and ginger in a blender.

2. Blend until smooth.
3. Divide the mixture into four to six glasses
4. Serve immediately.

Nutrition information: 250 calories, 2g fat, 0mg cholesterol, 14g carbohydrates, 2g protein, 35mg sodium.

77. Cranberry Zinger

Cranberry Zinger is a delicious, sweet and tart dessert perfect for summer days! This recipe is served in one large cake that is easy to make and an ideal addition to any summer get-together.

Serving: 8-10 | Preparation Time: 15 minutes | Ready Time: 1 hour

Ingredients:
- 2/3 cup all-purpose flour
- 1/3 cup granulated sugar
- 1 teaspoon baking powder
- 1/4 teaspoon salt
- 1/3 cup cranberry juice
- 2 tablespoons vegetable oil
- 2 eggs
- 2/3 cup fresh cranberries

Instructions:
1. Preheat oven to 350F. Grease a 9-inch square cake pan or 8-inch round cake pan.
2. In a medium bowl, mix together flour, sugar, baking powder, and salt. Make a well in the center and add cranberry juice, oil, and eggs; mix until blended.
3. Fold in cranberries and pour batter into prepared cake pan.
4. Bake for 30-35 minutes or until a toothpick inserted in the center comes out clean. Cool for 10 minutes before serving.

Nutrition information (per serving):

Calories: 140, Total Fat: 4 g, Saturated Fat: 1 g, Cholesterol: 30 mg, Sodium: 65 mg, Total Carbohydrate: 24 g, Dietary Fiber: 1 g, Sugars: 13 g, Protein: 3 g

78. Watermelon Granita

Watermelon Granita is a delicious and refreshing summer dessert. It's made with only a few simple ingredients, takes just minutes to prepare, and is full of sweet and fruity flavor.

Serves: 6 | Prep Time: 15 minutes | Ready Time: 4 hours

Ingredients:
- 4 cups chopped watermelon
- 2 tablespoons sugar
- 2 tablespoons fresh lime juice
-2 tablespoons fresh mint leaves, finely chopped

Instruction:
1. Using a blender or food processor, puree the watermelon until smooth.
2. Pour the puree into a 9-inch pan, add the sugar, and stir until combined.
3. Freeze for 3 hours or until almost solid. Use a fork to scrape the granita. Freeze another hour.
4. Remove the pan from the freezer, scoop out servings and place in small bowls.
5. Top with some fresh mint and enjoy cold.

Nutrition information: Calories: 46, Total Fat: 0g, Sodium: 5mg, Potassium: 106mg, Total Carbs: 11g, Dietary Fiber: 0g, Sugars: 7g, Protein: 0.9g.

79. Raspberry Coconut Cooler

This sweet and tart Raspberry Coconut Cooler is a delicious and refreshing summer cooler that will make you want more with every sip.

Serving: Serves 2-4 | Preparation Time: 10 minutes | Ready Time: 10 minutes

Ingredients:
- 2 cups fresh or frozen raspberries
- 2 cups cold coconut water
- 1 cup ice
- 2 tablespoons honey
- Juice of 1 lime

Instructions:
1. In a blender, combine the raspberries, coconut water, ice, honey, and lime juice.
2. Blend until smooth.
3. Divide the Raspberry Coconut Cooler among two to four glasses and enjoy!

Nutrition information: Per Serving (1/4 of total): 90 calories, 1.2g fat, 20.6g carbohydrates, 2.9g fiber, 16.6g sugar, 1.2g protein.

80. Orange Dream Punch

Orange Dream Punch is a light, refreshing combination of orange and pineapple flavors. This punch is perfect for summer BBQs or brunch gatherings with family and friends.

Serving: 12-15 | Preparation Time: 5 minutes | Ready Time: 15 minutes

Ingredients:
- 2 cans (11.5 oz each) Mandarins
- 1 can (46 oz) pineapple juice
- 8 oz frozen orange juice concentrate
- 2 cups of lemon lime soda
- 2 cups of sherbet
- Ice cubes

Instructions:

1. In a large pitcher or punch bowl mix together the mandarins, pineapple juice, and orange juice concentrate.
2. Mix in the lemon lime soda and stir to combine.
3. Place a scoop of sherbet into each glass.
4. Pour punch into each glass and top with a few ice cubes.

Nutrition information (per serving – 1 cup): 80 calories, 0.2 g of fat, 20 mg of sodium, 19.3 g of carb, 0.6 g of protein.

81. Fruity Sangria

Fruity Sangria is a delightful cocktail that combines sweet fruit and sparkling wine to produce a unique and luscious drink. It is perfect for parties and is sure to be a hit with any crowd!

Serving: 4-6 people; | Preparation Time: 10 minutes; | Ready Time: 10 minutes;

Ingredients:
- 750 ml bottle of sparkling Spanish rose wine
- 250 ml can of lemon-lime soda
- 2 oranges, sliced into wedges
- 2 lemons, sliced into wedges
- 2 peaches, diced
- 1/2 cup of raspberries
- Ice

Instructions:
1. In a large pitcher, combine the sparkling rose wine, lemon-lime soda, and citrus wedges.
2. Add in the diced peaches and raspberries.
3. Fill the pitcher with ice and stir to combine.
4. Serve and enjoy!

Nutrition information (per serving):
- Calories: 150
- Total fat: 0.5 g
- Sodium: 10 mg

- Total carbs: 22 g
- Dietary Fiber: 1 g
- Sugars: 18 g
- Protein: 0 g

82. Berry Breeze

Berry Breeze is a light and fresh summer dessert that is perfect for a hot day. It combines the sweet flavor of fresh berries and tangy yogurt, creating a cooling treat.

Serves 4. | Preparation Time: 10 minutes. | Ready Time: 25 minutes.

Ingredients:
- 2 cups fresh raspberries
- 1 1/2 cups Greek yoghurt
- 1/2 tsp ground cinnamon
- 1/4 cup honey
- Zest of 1 lemon

Instructions:
1. Begin by pureeing the raspberries in a blender or food processor until completely smooth.
2. Place pureed raspberries in a medium bowl and add the Greek yoghurt, cinnamon, honey, and lemon zest and stir until combined.
3. Divide the raspberry yogurt mixture among four bowls and place in the refrigerator to chill for 15 minutes.
4. Serve chilled.

Nutrition information (per serving):
- Calories: 185
- Fat: 1g
- Cholesterol: 0mg
- Sodium: 25mg
- Carbohydrates: 34g
- Fiber: 5g
- Sugar: 26g
- Protein: 10g

83. Spiced Apricot Refresher

This Spiced Apricot Refresher is a great way to cool off on a hot day, with a unique blend of fruity and spicy flavors. It's easy to make and perfect for both adults and children alike.

Serving: 4| Preparation Time: 10 minutes| Ready Time: 10 minutes

Ingredients:
- 2 cups apricot nectar, chilled
- 1 teaspoon honey
- 1/4 teaspoon ground cinnamon
- 1/8 teaspoon ground nutmeg
- 1/4 teaspoon ground ginger
- 4 fresh mint leaves, for garnish
- Ice cubes

Instructions:
1. In a medium bowl, combine chilled apricot nectar, honey, cinnamon, nutmeg and ginger.
2. Pour this mixture into four glasses filled with ice cubes.
3. Garnish with mint leaves and serve.

Nutrition information:
Calories: 64; Total Fat: 0 g; Saturated Fat: 0 g; Cholesterol: 0 mg; Sodium: 7.5 mg; Carbohydrates: 16 g; Protein: 0.6 g

84. Key Lime Pie

Key Lime Pie is an indulgent and tart dessert that is sure to satisfy any sweet tooth. Featuring a creamy key lime filling in a crunchy graham cracker crust, this dessert is bound to impress.

Serving: 6-8 slices| Preparation Time: 15 minutes| Ready Time: 4 hours

Ingredients:
- 2 tablespoons unsalted butter, melted
- 1 1/2 cups graham cracker crumbs
- 2 tablespoons granulated sugar
- 1/4 teaspoon salt
- 14-ounce can full-fat sweetened condensed milk
- 3 large eggs, separated
- 2/3 cup freshly-squeezed key lime juice (approximately 20 key limes)
- 2 teaspoons lime zest
- 2 tablespoons granulated sugar

Instructions:
1. Preheat the oven to 350F (177°C).
2. Combine butter, graham cracker crumbs, 2 tablespoons granulated sugar, and salt in a medium bowl.
3. Firmly press the mixture into the bottom of a 9-inch pie plate.
4. Bake for 10 minutes, until lightly browned.
5. Mix together sweetened condensed milk, egg yolks, lime juice and zest in a medium bowl. Pour into the baked crust.
6. Beat egg whites in a medium bowl until soft peaks form. Gradually beat in the remaining 2 tablespoons of sugar and continue beating until stiff peaks form.
7. Spoon the meringue onto the top of the pie, sealing it to the edges of the crust.
8. Bake for 15 minutes, or until the meringue is golden brown.
9. Let cool before serving.

Nutrition information (per serving): 242 calories, 12 g fat, 31 g carbohydrates, 3 g protein

85. Citrus Cooler

Citrus Cooler is a refreshingly light and zesty summer-time cooler. A combination of lemon, lime, and orange juices, ice, and sweet syrup come together to create a refreshing beverage perfect for warm days.

Serving: 4 | Preparation Time: 5 minutes | Ready Time: 5 minutes

Ingredients:
- 1/4 cup freshly squeezed lemon juice
- 1/4 cup freshly squeezed lime juice
- 1/4 cup freshly squeezed orange juice
- 2 tablespoons simple syrup
- 4 cups of ice

Instructions:
1. In a pitcher, combine lemon juice, lime juice, orange juice and simple syrup.
2. Add the ice and stir to combine.
3. Serve in glasses and enjoy!

Nutrition information (per serving):
Calories: 72, Total fat: 0 g, Carbohydrates: 17 g, Protein: 0 g, Sodium: 2 mg

86. Kiwi Margarita

Kiwi Margarita: A cool refresher on a summer night and an inventive twist on the classic margarita.

Serving: 1 | Preparation Time: 5 minutes | Ready Time: 5 minutes

Ingredients:
- 2 ounces tequila
- 1 ounce triple sec
- 2 kiwis
- 1 lime
- 2 teaspoons sugar
- Ice

Instructions:
1. In a blender or food processor, blend kiwis and sugar until smooth.
2. Squeeze juice from lime and add to kiwi mixture.
3. Add tequila and triple sec.

4. Add ice and blend until smooth.
5. Pour into a glass and enjoy!

Nutrition information: (per serving)
Calories: 142 kcal
Carbohydrates: 15g
Protein: 0.6g
Fat: 0.3g
Sugar: 12g

87. Margarita Punch

Margarita Punch is a light, refreshing cocktail that is easily served in a punch bowl with a mix of lime juice, orange liqueur, tequila, simple syrup and club soda. Perfect for summer get-togethers and Cinco de Mayo celebrations, this cocktail will be a hit at any party.

Serving: Makes 8-10 Servings | Preparation Time: 10 minutes | Ready Time: 10 minutes

Ingredients:
- 1 (12-ounce) can frozen limeade concentrate, thawed
- 6 ounces orange liqueur
- 6 ounces tequila
- 3 ounces simple syrup
- 2 (12-ounce) bottle club soda

Instructions:
1. In a large punch bowl, combine limeade concentrate, orange liqueur, tequila and simple syrup.
2. Stir to combine.
3. Add club soda and stir until combined.
4. Serve over ice.

Nutrition information: Per Serving: 100 calories; 0.5 g total fat; 40 mg sodium; 11 g carbohydrate; 10 g sugar.

88. Peach n' Cream

Peach n' Cream is a delicious, creamy and fruity dessert perfect for any occasion. This dish is perfect for bringing a bit of sweetness to your table.

Serving: 4 | Preparation Time: 10 minutes | Ready Time: 20 minutes

Ingredients:
- 2 cups peaches, peeled and chopped
- 1/3 cup sugar
- 2 tablespoons cornstarch
- Pinch of salt
- 2 cups heavy cream
- 1 teaspoon vanilla extract

Instructions:
1. In a small saucepan, combine the peaches, sugar, cornstarch and salt. Cook over medium-high heat, stirring often, until the mixture thickens and starts bubbling, about 5 minutes.
2. Reduce the heat to low and simmer for 3 minutes, stirring often.
3. In a separate bowl, combine the heavy cream and vanilla extract. Whip with an electric mixer until stiff peaks form.
4. Fold the whipped cream into the peach mixture in two batches, stirring well to combine.
5. Serve in individual bowls or glasses, or transfer to a serving bowl. Enjoy!

Nutrition information:
Calories: 299
Total Fat: 23 g
Saturated Fat: 14 g
Cholesterol: 85 mg
Sodium: 40 mg
Total Carbohydrates: 21 g
Dietary Fiber: 1 g
Sugars: 19 g
Protein: 3 g

89. Mango Sunrise

Mango Sunrise is a delicious and summery drink made with freshly squeezed mango juice, pineapple juice, and freshly cut oranges. It is a great addition to any brunch or cookouts on a hot summer day.

Serving: 4| Preparation Time: 10 Minutes

Ingredients
- 2 cups mango juice
- 1 cup pineapple juice
- 1 large orange cut into wedges
- 2 lime wedges
- Small amount of mint leaves

Instructions
1. In a large pitcher, combine the mango juice, pineapple juice and orange wedges.
2. Squeeze the lime wedges into the mixture and stir.
3. Slice a couple of mint leaves thinly and mix it into the juice.
4. Cover the pitcher and refrigerate for 10 minutes.
5. Serve the juice in individual glasses with extra lime wedges or mint leaves as a garnish.

Nutrition information
Per Serving: 165 Calories, 0g Fat, 44g Carbs, 0g Protein

90. Cranberry Swizzle

This Cranberry Swizzle is the perfect balance of sweet and tart. The combination of cranberry, lime, and orange juices make for a tart and flavorful drink that's great for all types of occasions.

Serving: Makes 4 drinks| Preparation Time: 5 minutes| Ready Time: 5 minutes

Ingredients:
•2 cups cranberry juice

- 1 cup lime juice
- 1/2 cup orange juice
- 1/4 cup simple syrup
- Ice cubes

Instructions:
1. In a pitcher, mix together the cranberry juice, lime juice, and orange juice.
2. Add simple syrup and stir to combine.
3. Fill a cocktail shaker with ice and add half of the drink mixture. Shake vigorously until well combined.
4. Pour the drink into four glasses and repeat steps 3-4 with the remaining half of the drink mixture.
5. Garnish with lime slices, if desired.

Nutrition information (per serving): 120 calories, 0.8g fat, 29g total carbohydrates, 1.4g protein.

91. Honeydew Limeade

This delicious, refreshing and zesty Honeydew Limeade is easy to make and perfect for a hot summer afternoon!

Serving- 4 | Preparation Time- 10 minutes

Ingredients:
- 2 cups pureed honeydew melon
- 1 cup freshly squeezed lime juice (approx. 8 limes)
- 1/2 cup sugar
- 4 cups cold water
- Garnish: slices of lime and honeydew melon

Instructions:
1. In a blender, mix together pureed melon, lime juice, and sugar until smooth.
2. In a large pitcher, combine the melon and lime juice mix with cold water. Stir until blended.

3. Serve over ice in individual glasses, and garnish with slices of lime and honeydew melon.

Nutrition information:
Per serving: 162 calories, 0g fat, 42g carbs, 0.9g protein, 27g sugar.

92. Apricot Fizz

This refreshing Apricot Fizz is the perfect summertime treat and a great way to cool off from the summer heat. With just a few simple and natural ingredients, this recipe can quickly become a summer favorite.

Serving: 2| Preparation Time: 10 minutes| Ready Time: 10 minutes

Ingredients:
- 4 ounces of apricot juice
- 2 ounces freshly-squeezed lime juice
- 2 ounces white sugar syrup
- 4 ounces soda water
- 1 apricot, sliced
- 2 lime wedges, for garnish

Instructions:
1. Start by combining the apricot juice, lime juice, and sugar syrup together in a shaker, with plenty of ice. Shake vigorously for around 15 to 20 seconds.
2. Strain the mixture into two chilled glasses and top with the soda water.
3. Garnish each with a lime wedge, fresh apricot slices, and a slice of lime.

Nutrition information (per serving):
Calories: 138, Total Fat: 0g, Sodium: 2mg, Total Carbohydrates: 35g, Sugars: 27g, Protein: 0g.

93. Lemon Coconut Refresher

Lemon Coconut Refresher is a light and refreshing drink perfect for a warm day. It's healthy and bursting with flavor, requiring just 4 simple ingredients. This recipe yields 2 servings, with a prep time of 5 minutes and a ready time of 5 minutes.

Serving: 2 | Preparation Time: 5 minutes | Ready Time: 5 minutes

Ingredients:
-4 tablespoons fresh lemon juice
-1-1/4 cup water
-2 tablespoons honey
-1 tablespoon coconut flakes

Instructions:
1. In a medium bowl, combine 4 tablespoons of fresh lemon juice, 1-1/4 cup of water, 2 tablespoons of honey and 1 tablespoon of coconut flakes.
2. Stir until the ingredients are thoroughly combined.
3. Pour the mixture into two glasses, serve over ice and garnish with a lemon slice and coconut flakes, if desired.

Nutrition information (per serving):
-Calories: 112 kcal
-Carbohydrates: 28 g
-Protein: 0 g
-Fat: 0 g

94. Fruity Freeze

Fruity Freeze is an easy-to-make frozen treat that's loaded with natural flavor and packed with antioxidants. It's a great way to cool off on a hot summer day and make a tasty snack.

Serving: Makes 4 servings | Preparation Time: 10 minutes | Ready Time: 20 minutes

Ingredients:
- 1/2 cup fresh or frozen strawberries

- 1/2 cup fresh or frozen blueberries
- 2 ripe bananas
- 1/4 cup honey
- Juice of 1 orange
- Pinch of cardamom (optional)
- Pinch of ground cinnamon (optional)

Instructions:
1. Place strawberries, blueberries, bananas, honey, orange juice, cinnamon, and cardamom in a blender.
2. Blend until smooth and completely puréed.
3. Pour the mixture into a 9x9 inch glass dish.
4. Cover the top of the dish with cling wrap.
5. Place the dish in the freezer for 15 minutes, or until it has frozen.
6. Once frozen, take the dish out of the freezer and cut the Fruity Freeze into cubes.
7. Serve and enjoy!

Nutrition information:
Calories: 100; Fat: 0.2g; Carbohydrates: 25.3g; Protein: 1.3g; Fiber: 2.7g; Sugar: 18.9g

95. Green Apple Slush

Green Apple Slush is an easy and refreshing frozen beverage perfect for summer days and outdoor gatherings. With a few simple ingredients and a few minutes of your time, you can whip up this tasty beverage in no time.

Serving: 4 | Preparation Time: 10 minutes | Ready Time: 10 minutes

Ingredients:
- 4 large granny smith apples
- 2/3 cup granulated sugar
- 2 tablespoons freshly-squeezed lemon juice
- 2 cups cold water
- 3 cups ice cubes

Instructions:
1. Peel and core the apples, then chop them into small pieces.
2. Place the apples pieces in a medium saucepan over medium-high heat.
3. Add the sugar and lemon juice, then stir well to combine.
4. Reduce the heat to medium and cook, stirring constantly, until the apples are soft and the mixture thickens, about 8 minutes.
5. Remove from heat and let cool.
6. Place cooled apple mixture into a blender and add cold water and ice cubes.
7. Blend until smooth.
8. Serve immediately in chilled glasses.

Nutrition information: Per serving (1 cup): Calories: 145, Total Fat: 0 g, Cholesterol: 0 mg, Sodium: 2 mg, Total Carbohydrates: 36 g, Protein: 0.9 g.

96. Raspberry Peach Slush

Introducing Raspberry Peach Slush, a delicious, fruity slush that is sure to be a favorite on hot summer days! This refreshing beverage requires just a few simple ingredients, and is both easy and quick to make.

Serving: 4 | Preparation Time: 5 mins | Ready Time: 5 mins

Ingredients:
- 4 cups of frozen unsweetened peaches
- 2 tablespoons of agave nectar
- 1/2 cup of raspberry juice
- 2 cups of ice
- 1/2 cup of fresh or frozen raspberries

Instructions:
1. In a blender, add the frozen peaches, agave nectar, and raspberry juice. Blend on high speed until smooth.
2. Add the ice and raspberries and blend until the ice is fully crushed.
3. Serve in individual glasses and top with fresh raspberries, if desired.

Nutrition information: Per Serving: Calories- 111 Carbohydrates- 28.5g Sugar- 22g Sodium- 3mg Fat- 0.5g Protein- 1g

97. Banana Colada

Banana Colada is an incredibly creamy and delicious tropical drink that's perfect for enjoying a hot afternoon or toasting a special celebration. It's easy to make and uses just a few ingredients to make a delicious beverage sure to please any crowd.

Serving: 1 drink| Preparation Time: 5 minutes| Ready Time: 5 minutes

Ingredients:
- 2 ounces Rum
- 1 banana
- 2 ounces coconut milk
- 2 ounces pineapple juice
- Crushed ice
- Whipped cream (optional)
- Pineapple slices (optional)

Instructions:
1. Place the banana and rum in a blender and blend until it is pureed.
2. Add the coconut milk, pineapple juice, and crushed ice to the blender and blend until combined.
3. Pour into a glass and top with whipped cream and pineapple slices, if desired.

Nutrition information: 200 calories, 10 g fat, 16 g carbohydrates, 0 g protein

98. Pomegranate Punch

Pomegranate Punch is a tasty and refreshing beverage perfect for any occasion. Bursting with flavor and natural sweetness, made with pomegranate and other delicious ingredients, this punch is sure to be a hit.

Serving: 8 | Preparation Time: 10 minutes | Ready Time: 10 minutes

Ingredients:
- 8 cups pomegranate juice
- 1/2 cup fresh lime juice
- 2 cups ginger ale
- 2 tablespoons superfine sugar
- 8 strips of lime peel

Instructions:
1. In a large jug, stir together the pomegranate juice, lime juice, ginger ale, and superfine sugar until well blended.
2. Add the lime peel strips.
3. Refrigerate the punch for 2 hours.
4. Serve chilled in glasses with a piece of the lime peel.

Nutrition information: per serving: 56 calories; 0.2 g fat; 14.7 g carbohydrates; 0.3 g protein.

CONCLUSION

Concluding our review of the 98 Refreshing Mocktail Recipes cookbook, we can say that this cookbook provides a great variety of delicious and non-alcoholic drinks for any occasion. Whether you are looking for a more sophisticated option for a romantic evening, or an easy and tasty summertime thirst-quencher, this cookbook has you covered. With such an expansive range of flavors, everyone can find something to their liking in here.

Furthermore, many of the recipes contain elements of seasonality and freshness, not only in terms of ingredients, but also when it comes to their method of preparation. The recipes are straightforward and easy to follow, with most of them taking up to fifteen minutes to prepare. All in all, the 98 Refreshing Mocktail Recipes cookbook provides a great wealth of options to create delicious drinks, without a lot of fuss.

These drinks are perfect for any gathering, be it with friends, family, or a romantic night out. They provide an excellent alternative to alcohol, and have a refreshing, unique flavor that will surely represent the occasion. Moreover, this cookbook provides the ideal opportunity to experiment in the kitchen, with a wide array of delicious recipes to choose from. This cookbook is definitely worth a look, and will surely provide you with plenty of delicious and refreshing drink options for every occasion.